EXPLORING APPLESOFT

Roger McShane

Prentice-Hall of Australia

A Prentice-Hall Direct Edition

© 1983 by Prentice-Hall of Australia Pty Ltd

Prentice-Hall of Australia Pty Ltd, Sydney
Prentice-Hall International Inc., London
Prentice-Hall Canada Inc., Toronto
Prentice-Hall of India Private Ltd, New Delhi
Prentice-Hall of Japan Inc., Tokyo
Prentice-Hall of Southeast Asia Pte Ltd, Singapore
Editora Prentice-Hall do Brasil LTDA., Rio de Janeiro
Whitehall Books Ltd, Wellington
Prentice-Hall Inc., Englewood Cliffs, New Jersey

1 2 3 4 5 87 86 85 84 83

Printed and bound in Australia by
Globe Press Pty Ltd, Brunswick, Victoria

Cover by Sam Latsis

Apple II and APPLESOFT are registered
trademarks of Apple Computer, Inc.

ISBN 0-13-295916-X

Library of Congress Cataloguing in Publication Data

McShane, Roger, 1950-
  Exploring Applesoft.

  Includes index.
  1. Apple II (Computer)--Programming. 2. Apple IIe
(Computer)--Programming. I. Title.
Qa76.8.A662M4 1983   001.64'2   83-11152
ISBN 0-13-295916-X

National Library of Australia
Cataloguing-in-Publication Data

McShane, Roger.
  Exploring APPLESOFT.

  Includes index.
  ISBN 0 7248 0417 X.

  1. Apple II (Computer) - Programming.
  I. Title

001.64'24

CONTENTS

PREFACE

This book has been written in response to the needs of three groups: students having their first contact with a microcomputer, students who wish to study programming as an interest rather than a discipline, and last, but by no means least, adults who find the traditional approaches to programming to be difficult or confusing.

The main philosophy behind the approach taken in this book is that students will grasp programming concepts more readily if they can 'see' the results of their programs. For this reason there is a heavy emphasis on the use of graphics throughout the book. The author believes that students are able to detect errors, and correct those errors, much faster if they have a graphics image to deal with.

Another variation from the traditional approach is that the syntax of the APPLESOFT language is introduced incidentally. The author believes that many students are given a very bad impression of programming in their first few lessons when a bewildering number of 'rules' for PRINT formatting or mathematical formulae are thrust upon them. The time for an explanation of these facts is when the student needs to use them - if they are comfortable in using the computer for simple programming they will be more receptive to looking up the rules in books and manuals.

The book has been designed to appeal to a wide range of students and therefore does not contain many examples or exercises from the mathematics area. Computers are used widely in the general community for accounting, word processing, file handling, record keeping, information sharing and for recreation - very few people use them for mathematics in the true sense and the author believes that the teaching of programming should reflect this.

In the first sections of the book a number of 'programming models' have been introduced to help explain some of the elementary programming concepts which are so often dealt with in a cursory fashion. It is the author's belief that students begin writing programs by imitating sections of code that they have already seen. It is not until they have internalized a complete set of 'models' that they become proficient at the task of coding. One of the chief responsibilities of the teacher, therefore, is to provide students with an adequate set of models. Conversely, students should not be asked to attempt problems for which adequate models have not been provided.

The book has been divided into a number of lessons each with a particular theme, and these are supplemented by a number of 'interludes' and appendices which contain much of the technical information the students will need. Most of the lessons finish with a slightly longer program. It will not be necessary for all students to understand those programs as the next lesson will begin at an easier level in each case. The author has included these harder examples for those students who find programming to be easy. Towards the end of the book a number of programming standards are introduced to show students who intend to take their study of programming further that adherence to standards and programming style is essential in the programming field.

I would like to pay a tribute to my wife Ann and my children Stuart and Sallyanne who have supported me in the development of this book, giving up many weekends and holidays so that the project could be completed. My sincere thanks are also extended to Scott Brownell who has been an inspiration to all computer educators in Tasmania, and to Jo Ginn for the diagrams used in this book.

Roger McShane

Hobart, 1983.

Lesson 1

Graphics Programming

In this lesson the fundamental concepts of computer programming will be discussed. These ideas will be introduced by plotting various images on the Apple's graphics display. The fundamental ideas of assigning values to variables and constructing loops and branches are introduced.

Our investigation of the way to program the Apple microcomputer will begin with a look at the GRAPHICS features. The Apple must first be turned on. Throughout these lessons it will be assumed that the Apple has been turned on and Applesoft is the standard language. The prompt] will appear as soon as Applesoft is available.

The Apple can display TEXT (ordinary characters) or GRAPHICS (pictures and designs) or a mixture of both. One of the graphics screens (the low-resolution) will be displayed in response to the instruction:

    ] GR

All of the screen, except for the bottom four lines, will be cleared to prepare for the graphics display.   The graphics display consists of 1600 points on the screen made up of 40 columns (numbered 0 to 39) and 40 rows (also numbered 0 to 39).   The top left hand corner is numbered 0,0.

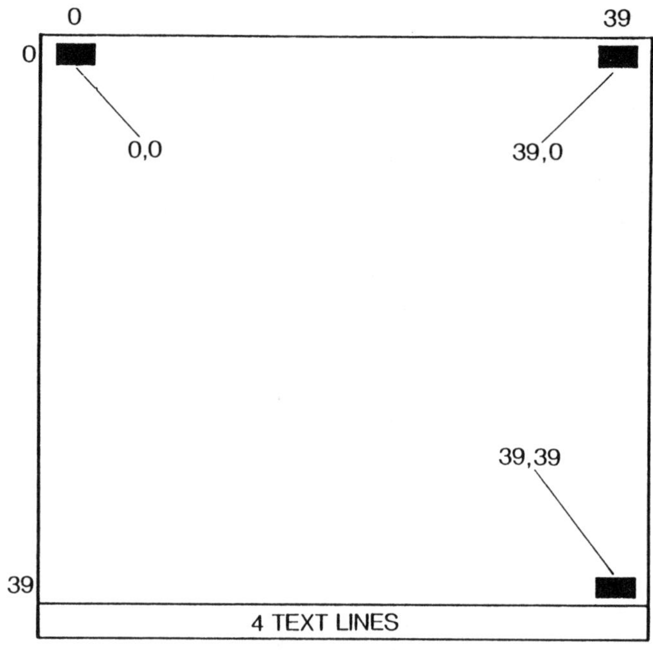

LOW-RESOLUTION GRAPHICS DISPLAY

Graphics points are displayed using the PLOT command.   Try
the instruction:

    ] PLOT 5,30

This instruction asks the Apple to display a point in the
5th column and the 30th row.   After we have typed this
instruction, however, nothing will be seen!   The reason
for this is that the Apple must know what COLOR to plot the
point in. We have just plotted a black point on a black
background.

The COLOR can be specified by typing

    ] COLOR=2

If we now repeat the instruction

    ] PLOT 5,30

a small, colored rectangle will appear on the left-hand
side of the screen towards the bottom.   The color codes
are:

    0..... BLACK   8..... BROWN
    1..... MAGENTA   9..... ORANGE
    2..... DARK BLUE   10..... GRAY
    3..... PURPLE   11..... PINK
    4..... DARK GREEN   12..... LIGHT GREEN
    5..... GRAY   13..... YELLOW
    6..... MEDIUM BLUE   14..... AQUA
    7..... LIGHT BLUE   15..... WHITE

These colors will vary from one TV set or monitor to
another.Try some different COLOR commands such as COLOR=9
or COLOR=12. Follow the COLOR commands with PLOT commands.

Throughout this book a number of PROGRAMMING MODELS will be
provided to act as a guide for using various statements in
your own programs.

MODEL 1

A point is PLOTted in the current color according to the column and row which it is given.

        PLOT 5,2

In the example given, the point will be plotted in the fifth column and the second row.

. . . .

Exercises

(a) Photostat the diagram of the low-resolution graphics display then mark in each of the PLOT commands.

(i)   PLOT 0,0   (ii)   PLOT 3,18   (iii) PLOT 37,23
(iv)   PLOT 1,5   (v)   PLOT 17,15   (vi) PLOT 39,20
(vii) PLOT 20,39   (viii) PLOT 0,5   (xi) PLOT 0,39
(x)   PLOT 15,10   (xi)   PLOT 20,30   (xii) PLOT 19,39

(b) Draw the outline of a yacht on a graphics sheet then write down the PLOT commands required to draw it.

(c) Teacher activity:

     Pass out a graphics sheet to each student then call out a number of PLOT commands. For marking purposes pass around an overhead projector transparency with the correct positions marked on it. The student places this over his or her own answer to check.

. . . .

If we now wish to display a point then erase it, the
following sequence of commands could be typed in:

```
] GR                 ..... display graphics screen
] COLOR=15           ..... set color to white
] PLOT 15,30         ..... plot a point in white
] COLOR=0            ..... set color to black
] PLOT 15,30         ..... point disappears
```

If we wish to plot a point, then erase it, then plot it at
the next position and hence move the point across the
screen it would be very tedious to type these commands in.
This is because we are giving our commands to the Apple in
what is known as IMMEDIATE MODE.   An alternative method is
to STORE a sequence of instructions (known as a PROGRAM)
and then ask the computer to execute these instructions.
A program to display a point would look like this:

```
] 10 GR
] 20 COLOR=4
] 30 PLOT 15,30
] 40 END
```

After typing these instructions you will notice that
nothing has been displayed.   This is because we have used
line numbers (10, 20 etc.) to store the sequence of
instructions (program) in the Apple's memory.   To activate
the sequence of instructions type the following:

```
] RUN
```

The point will now be displayed.   If RUN is typed again
the point will be displayed again and so on.   To erase
this program and start a NEW one type:

```
] NEW
```

Now you will notice that the program "disappears"
underneath the graphics screen.   When a program is being
typed it is a good idea to return to TEXT mode by typing:

```
] TEXT
```

At this stage you will notice that the display looks very
strange.   If you wish to remove this, press RETURN a
number of times.

The following program will display an orange dot in each
corner of the screen:

```
] 10 GR              ..... display graphics
] 20 COLOR=9         ..... set orange
] 30 PLOT 0,0        ..... top left
] 40 PLOT 39,0       ..... top right
] 50 PLOT 39,39      ..... bottom right
] 60 PLOT 0,39       ..... bottom left
```

To activate this set of instructions remember to type:

```
] RUN
```

Notice that it is <u>not</u> necessary to reset the COLOR after each PLOT command.

At the end of this lesson there is a program which causes a "ball" to bounce off the edge of the screen. What are the instructions needed to do this? Let us first look at the set of instructions which display a point and then erase it:

```
] 10 GR
] 20 COLOR=15
] 30 PLOT 15,30
] 40 COLOR=0
] 50 PLOT 15,30
] 60 END
```

Now type:

```
] RUN
```

You will notice that the point hardly appeared. This is because the Apple executes the instructions very quickly. If we wish to slow the Apple down a bit, a good idea is to "waste" some time in between instructions. One way of doing this is to make the APPLE "count" to a large number such as 100 or 500 or 1000. The Apple does this with the following "magic" command (which shall be explained later):

```
] FOR I = 1 TO 100 : NEXT I
```

Therefore we could amend the previous program by typing

```
] 35 FOR I = 1 TO 100 : NEXT I
```

This would have the effect of inserting the counting instruction between lines 30 and 40.   Now when RUN is typed a white dot will be plotted and will remain while the Apple counts to 100.   Increase this value to 300 or 500 if you wish the dot to stay there longer.

Let us now write a program to move the point across the screen at a rate we can see.   Before this is done the concept of a VARIABLE must be understood.   In the memory of any computer there are a large number of memory "cells" (variables) set aside to store numbers of characters. Study the next four programming models carefully before going on to the next program.

. . . .

MODEL 2

A memory cell or VARIABLE should be INITIALIZED (i.e. given a first value) before being used. The basket of apples will be used to represent the variable called APPLES. Some microcomputers, including the Apple, set all variables to 0 when RUN is typed. It is good programming practice, however, to give them an initial value.   Notice that the cell has a name (LABEL) as well as a VALUE.

      100 APPLES=0 .....   put 0 in the cell
                                     labelled APPLES

. . . .

MODEL 3

Numbers can be stored in VARIABLES. We say that the VALUE of 3 has been assigned to the VARIABLE called APPLES. Notice that there are three apples in the basket.

```
200 APPLES=3
```

MODEL 4

The value of a variable can be increased or decreased. In this example we say that "the variable APPLES is assigned the old value of the variable plus 1". In this case there were three apples in the basket, now there are four.

```
30 APPLES = APPLES + 1
```

MODEL 5

A set of instructions can be executed over and over again
through the use of a LOOP.   Normally a program is executed
line by line - the GOTO statement allows a change to a
different part of the program.

     90 GOTO 30 .....   go back to line 30

The program to move a point across the screen can now be
developed :

] 10 GR	..... turn graphics on
] 20 COLUMN=0	..... set column value
] 30 COLOR=15	..... set color value
] 40 PLOT COLUMN, 20	..... plot first point
] 50 FOR I = 1 TO 100:NEXT I	..... wait a while
] 60 COLOR=0	..... set color to black
] 70 PLOT COLUMN, 20	..... erase point
] 80 COLUMN=COLUMN + 1	..... move to next column
] 90 GOTO 30	..... do it again

When execution reaches line 90 it will simply jump back up
to line 30 and start there again.   When the command RUN is

issued, the white dot will move across the screen and then
the message:

> ? ILLEGAL QUANTITY ERROR IN 40

will be displayed.   The reason for this is that the
variable COLUMN has taken the values 0,1,2,3, ... and so
on, and has finally reached the value 40.   There is no
value 40, however, so the Apple has become confused! After
the set of exercises, a method of testing the value of
variables will be introduced. The test will help eliminate
this error.

. . . .

Exercises

(a) Make the dot move across the screen very slowly.

(b) Make the dot move across the top of the screen.

(c) Make the dot move across the bottom of the screen.
     Note: it is not necessary to retype the whole
     program, just retype the lines which need changing.

(d) Change the program so that the dot moves down the
     screen in the center.   Hint: change the variable from
     COLUMN to ROW and change the PLOT command to PLOT
     20,ROW.

(e) Make the dot move down the screen on the left hand
     side.

(f) Make the dot change color each time it is plotted.

(g) Make the dot move across the screen, but this time
     only plot it every second point.

(h) Make the dot move diagonally from the top left hand
     corner to the bottom right hand corner.   Increase a
     COLUMN variable and a ROW variable.

(i) Make the dot move from the top right hand corner to
     the bottom left hand corner.

. . . .

MODEL 6

The value of a variable can be <u>TESTED</u>. If it passes the
test then one set of instructions will be executed,
otherwise a different set will be executed.

Example 1:
```
10 APPLES = 2
20 IF APPLES = 2 THEN APPLES = 0
```

In this example the value of the variable APPLES is
initially 2 therefore the instruction after the THEN
statement will be executed. Therefore the value of APPLES
is now 0.

Example 2:
```
10 APPLES = 1
20 IF APPLES = 2 THEN APPLES = 0
```

In this example the value of APPLES is not 2 so the
instructions after the THEN statement will be ignored.

The error message can be stopped by "testing" to see if the
point has reached the edge of the screen. This is done by
introducing the following line:

     ] 85 IF COLUMN = 40 THEN END

This instruction tests to see if the variable COLUMN has
the value 40 stored in it.   If it does not, then the
instruction is ignored and execution continues on line 90.
If it does then the program ENDs.   If you wish to make the
point continue forever then use the instruction:

     ] 85 IF COLUMN = 40 THEN COLUMN = 0

Once the value of COLUMN is changed to 0 execution will
continue at line 90.   This program will continue forever
or until the control button and the letter C are pressed
together (written as CTRL-C).

As a final program in this chapter we will think of the
point as a "ball" which we wish to bounce off the edge of
the screen.   We will also make two further changes. From
now on the prompt] will be dropped and the colon (:) will
be used to separate commands on the same line as a way of
saving space.

First, type the command NEW to erase the previous program.

```
 10 GR                        ..... turn graphics on
 20 COLUMN = 30               ..... start at column 30
 30 COLOR = 15                ..... color white
 40 PLOT COLUMN, 20           ..... plot the point
 50 FOR I = 1 TO 100 :
        NEXT I                ..... wait
 60 COLOR = 0                 ..... color black
 70 PLOT COLUMN, 20           ..... erase point
 80 COLUMN = COLUMN + 1       ..... move right
 90 IF COLUMN=40 THEN 200     ..... edge of screen
100 GOTO 30                   ..... do it again
200 COLOR = 15               ..... color white
210 COLUMN = COLUMN - 1       ..... move left
220 PLOT COLUMN, 20           ..... plot the point
230 FOR I = 1 TO 100 :
        NEXT I                ..... wait a while
240 COLOR = 0                 ..... color black
250 PLOT COLUMN, 20           ..... erase point
260 IF COLUMN=30 THEN 30      ..... start again
270 GOTO 200                  ..... do this bit again
```

This program is very inefficient because the part which moves the ball left and the part which moves the ball right are almost identical and do not need to be separated if some programming tricks are used. At this point, however, the programming concepts need to be learned not the tricks.

. . . .

Exercises

(a) Write a program which will draw a straight horizontal line on the screen.   Note: there is an Applesoft command -HLIN- which does this, but it is best avoided because of its confusing structure.

(b) Write a program which will draw a short, vertical line in the top left hand corner of the screen.

(c) Draw a white border around the screen.

(d) Draw a square in the center of the screen.   Do not worry if it doesn't look like a square - the points are rectangular rather than square.

(e) Write a program to draw a diagonal line on the screen, from the top left hand corner to the bottom right hand corner.

(f) Repeat (e) but this time draw the line from the top right hand corner to the bottom left hand corner of the screen.

(g) Extend (e) and (f) so that a large X is displayed.

(h) Write a program which will draw a white square with a red triangle on top of it.

(i) Extend (h) so that a house is displayed by drawing some doors and windows.

(j) The final program in this lesson shows how to bounce a ball off the side of the screen. Extend the program so that the screen acts like a billiard table with the ball bouncing around the screen like a billiard ball.

(k) Draw the engine of a train with some smoke pouring out of the chimney.

. . . .

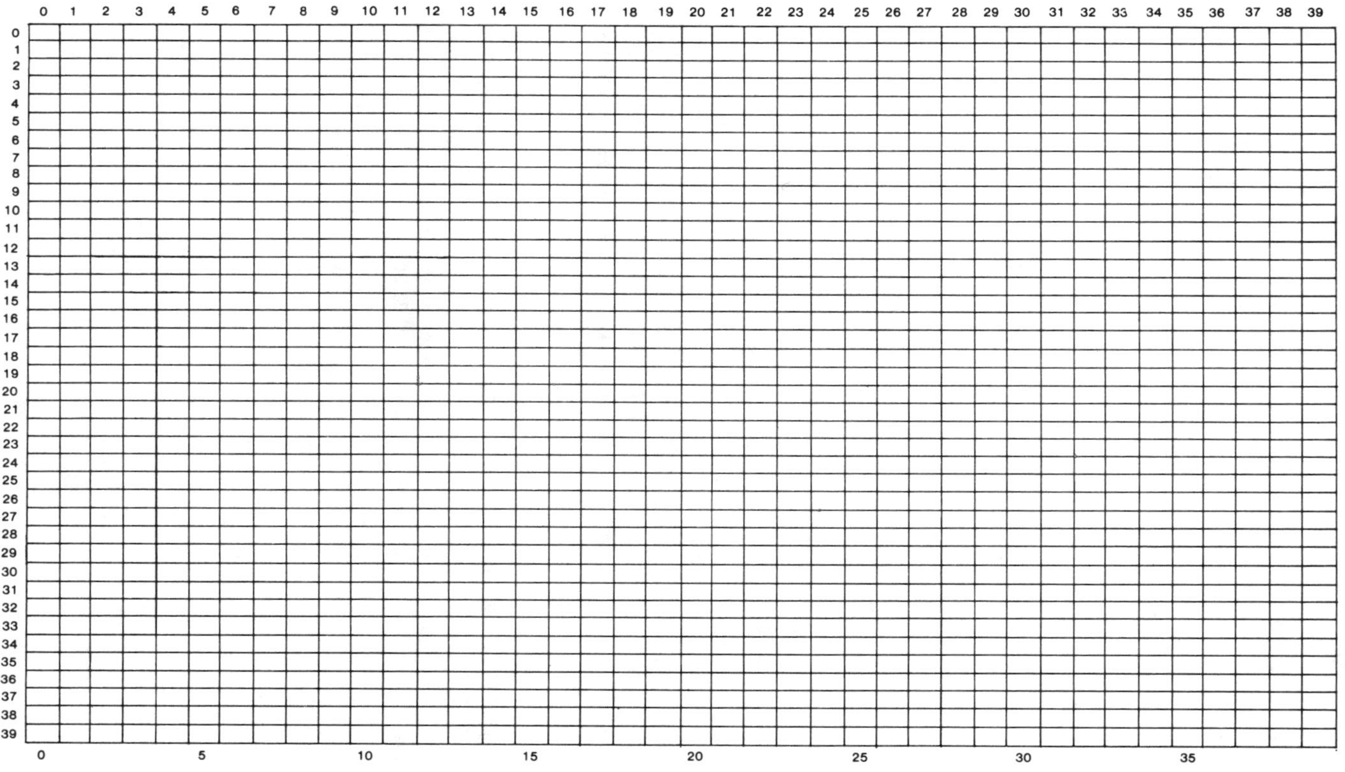

LOW - RESOLUTION PLANNING SHEET

Interlude 1

1. To display the low-resolution graphics screen type GR.
    To return to the text screen to view the program type
    TEXT.

2. To view a program when in TEXT display type

    LIST

    If only one line needs to be displayed type LIST
    followed by the line number e.g. LIST 20.   Other
    useful options are :

    LIST 100,130

    this lists all lines from 100 to 130 inclusive.

    LIST 100,

    lists from line 100 to the end of the program.

    LIST,100

    lists from the beginning of the program to line 100.

    To stop a long program "scrolling" off the screen type
    CTRL-S (hold the control button down and press the S).
    To resume scrolling, type CTRL-S again. To stop the
    program LISTing altogether, type CTRL-C.

3. MORE ABOUT VARIABLES

    It has already been stated that variables are "cells"
    in the computer's memory with a LABEL and a VALUE. The
    labels can be any collection of characters, up to 238
    long, which begin with a letter. Only the first two
    characters, however, are used to identify the
    variable. Therefore VAN and VAMPIRE would be regarded
    as the same variable by Applesoft. Another problem is
    that Applesoft "knows" a number of words called
    RESERVED words. Some of these reserved words we have
    already come across are: GR, END, IF, THEN, PLOT,
    COLOR, GOTO, FOR, NEXT. These reserved words MUST NOT
    appear in variable names.   Therefore the variable
    names GRAPE and FORUM would be illegal as they contain
    the reserved words GR and FOR respectively.

4.   LINE NUMBERS

Line numbers are usually started at, say, 100 and then
increased by 10 or 20 or 100 for each subsequent line.
The reason for this is that if a line is missed out
then it can be inserted between the two line numbers
as required.   For example:

        100   GR
        120   PLOT 5,20
        110   COLOR=15

would cause line 110 to be inserted between line 100
and line 120.

Lesson 2

Further Graphics Programming

The ideas which were introduced in lesson 1 are now used to draw images on the high-resolution screen. The use of variables is extended, particularly in relation to the HPLOT statement, and FOR loops are treated in more detail.

The Apple has another way of displaying graphics - known as HIGH-RESOLUTION GRAPHICS. In low-resolution graphics 1600 points could be plotted in 40 columns and 40 rows. In high-resolution 44800 points (which are obviously much finer) can be plotted in 280 columns and 160 rows.

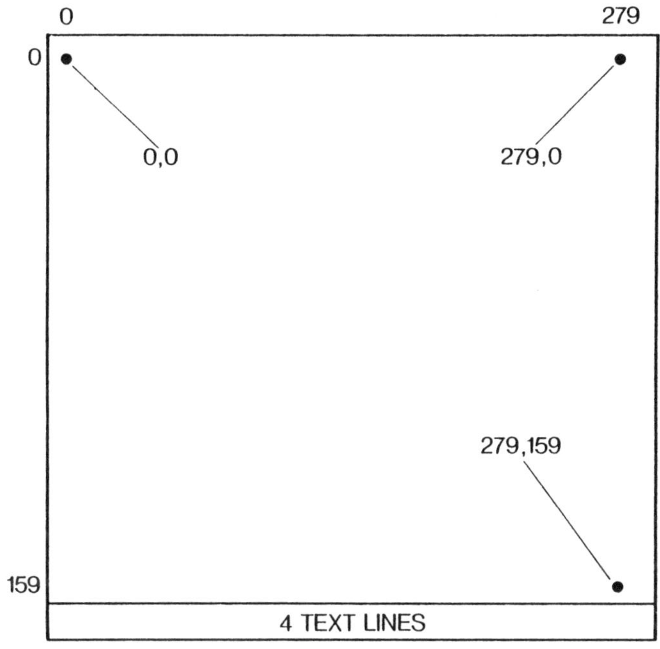

HIGH-RESOLUTION GRAPHICS DISPLAY

The commands are very similar to those used in lesson 1.

    HGR   .....   turn on, and clear, the high-
                       resolution graphics screen.

    HCOLOR   .....   set the high-resolution color

    HPLOT   .....   plot a point

Eight colors can be selected as shown in the following
table.

    0..... BLACK   4..... BLACK

    1..... GREEN   5..... ?

    2..... BLUE   6..... ?

    3..... WHITE   7..... WHITE

Colors 5 and 6 vary from one television monitor to another.
Notice that there are two numbers for white and two numbers
for black.

The HPLOT statement is more powerful than the PLOT
statement in that it can be used to plot horizontal,
vertical or diagonal lines. For example:

    HPLOT 1,30 TO 20,30

will plot a short horizontal line in the top left hand
corner of the screen. To see this line enter the following
program:

    10 HGR   ..... turn on, and clear,
                                      the high-resolution
                                      graphics screen.
    20 HCOLOR=7   ..... set white
    30 HPLOT 1,30 TO 20,30   ..... plot the line
    40 END

Now type

RUN

and the high resolution graphics screen will be cleared and the line displayed. Now type:

TEXT

Notice that the program has remained on the screen "behind" the graphics display. Other examples of using the HPLOT statement are:

        HPLOT 140,20 TO 140,150

which will plot a long vertical line in column 140; and

        HPLOT 200,10 TO 200,30

which will plot a short vertical line in column 200;
and
        HPLOT 0,80 TO 279,80

which will plot a horizontal line across the middle of the screen; and

        HPLOT 100,80 TO 140,80 TO 140,120 TO 100,120
            TO 100,80

which will plot a square. Notice that the TO command can be used many times.

Now let us see how the HPLOT statement can be used to draw a border around the screen. Although it can be done with one HPLOT statement, four will be used so that each line can be explained separately.

```
100 HGR:HCOLOR=7
110 HPLOT 0,0 TO 279,0        ..... top line
120 HPLOT 279,0 TO 279,159    ..... right side
130 HPLOT 279,159 TO 0,159    ..... bottom line
140 HPLOT 0,159 TO 0,0        ..... left side
150 END
```

This program was easy to plan because the coordinates of the corners of the screen are well known. In most cases, however, it is necessary to use the high-resolution graphics planning sheet which is at the end of this lesson. If we wish to display a large letter E in the middle of the screen, we will need to draw it on the sheet first and then work out the coordinates.

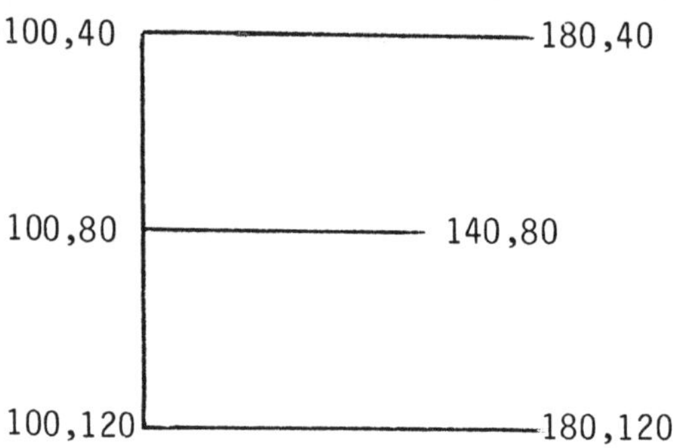

The program starts at the top right corner of the letter E.

```
100 HGR: HCOLOR=7
110 HPLOT 180,40 TO 100,40
120 HPLOT 100,40 TO 100,120
130 HPLOT 100,120 TO 180,120
140 HPLOT 100,80 TO 140,80
150 END
```

The program could be shortened to:

```
100 HGR: HCOLOR=7
110 HPLOT 180,40 TO 100,40 TO 100,120 TO 180,120
120 HPLOT 100,80 TO 140,80
130 END
```

Many of the following exercises will require careful planning before the program is written.

. . . .

Exercises

(a) Plot a horizontal line which is 100 points long, in the middle of the screen.

(b) Plot a similar horizontal line in the bottom left hand corner of the screen.

(c) Plot a short vertical line in the bottom left hand corner of the screen.

(d) Plot a vertical line in the top right hand corner of the screen.

(e)   Plot a vertical line down the center of the screen.

(f)   Plot a horizontal line across the center of the screen.

(g)   Draw the following shape with one HPLOT statement.

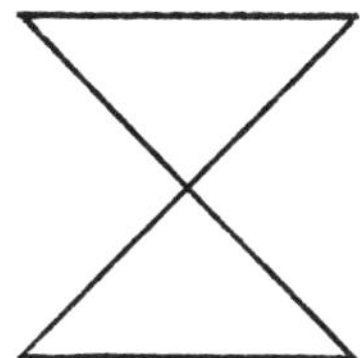

(h)   Draw a large X on the graphics screen.

(i)   Draw the following letters on the screen:

        A, E, F, H, I, H, Z

(j)   Write a program to draw your own initials.

(k)   Draw the following shapes on the screen:

        house, robot, yacht, train, wagon, chair

(l)   Convert the last program in lesson 1 so that a small
      ball bounces off the edge of the high-resolution
      screen.

. . . .

So far, variables have not been used in the HPLOT
statements. The use of variables provides more flexibility
in the displays we wish to produce. To draw a square in
the middle of the screen we could use the following
program:

```
100 HGR
110 HCOLOR=7
120 HPLOT 120,60 TO 160,60       ..... top
130 HPLOT 160,60 TO 160,100      ..... right
140 HPLOT 160,100 TO 120,100     ..... bottom
150 HPLOT 120,100 TO 120,60      ..... left
```

A square with a side of 40 will be drawn. If we wish to
draw a square with a different side, however, all the HPLOT
statements must be changed. To overcome this problem,
VARIABLES can be used within the HPLOT statement. For
example, the following program segment will draw a line
from 40,100 to 130,100:


```
100 HGR
110 HCOLOR=7
120 A=40 : B=130
130 HPLOT A,100 TO B,100
```

This idea can now be used to rewrite the program which
draws a square. The variable SIDE will be used to hold the
length of the side of the square.


```
100 HGR
110 HCOLOR=7
120 SIDE=30
130 HPLOT 120,60 TO 120+SIDE,60
140 HPLOT 120+SIDE,60 TO 120+SIDE,60
150 HPLOT 120+SIDE,60+SIDE TO 120,60+SIDE
160 HPLOT 120,60+SIDE TO 120,60
```

Now only line 120 needs to be changed if the length of the
side is to be changed. The next problem is that the top
left hand corner of the square will always be at 120,60.
To overcome this problem, use two variables for the
coordinates of that corner.


```
100 HGR : HCOLOR=7
110 X=20                 ..... X value of corner
120 Y=50                 ..... Y value of corner
130 SIDE=40              ..... length of side
140 HPLOT X,Y TO X+SIDE,Y
150 HPLOT X+SIDE,Y TO X+SIDE,Y+SIDE
160 HPLOT X+SIDE,Y+SIDE TO X,Y+SIDE
170 HPLOT X,Y+SIDE TO X,Y
```


Now a square of any side can be placed anywhere on the
screen by changing lines 110 to 130. (NOTE: BE CAREFUL NOT
TO GIVE VALUES WHICH WILL NOT FIT ON THE SCREEN.)

The next step is to alter the value of the variables inside
a loop. First study the following models carefully.

MODEL 7

The 'counting loop' which was introduced in the first chapter can be used to assign a number of successive values to a VARIABLE.

For example:

10 FOR APPLES=1 TO 10

20 NEXT APPLES

will successively
assign the values
1 to 10 to the cell
called APPLES.

Imagine picking apples from a tree. The basket will have one apple, then two apples, then three apples and so on.

The counting loop also allows more than one apple to be picked at a time by using a STEP statement.

10 FOR APPLES=0 TO 10 STEP 2

20 NEXT APPLES

will cause the values 0,2,4
etc. to be assigned to the
cell labelled APPLES.

. . . .

MODEL 8

A variable can be used in an HPLOT statement to cause a
number of lines to be drawn. The following example draws
five horizontal lines:

```
5 HGR : HCOLOR=7

10 FOR ROW=1 TO 5

20     HPLOT 0,ROW TO 50,ROW

30 NEXT ROW
```

To draw vertical lines alter
the X coordinate.

```
10 FOR CLMN=1 TO 5

20     HPLOT CLMN,0 TO CLMN,50

30 NEXT CLMN
```

. . . .

Let us now use these models to construct a colored square.

```
100 HGR : HCOLOR=2
110 FOR ROW=80 TO 140
120     HPLOT 120,ROW TO 180,ROW
130 NEXT ROW
```

Line 110 determines that the square will be constructed
from 60 lines and the HPLOT statement ensures that the
lines will be 60 points wide (i.e. 120 to 180). Experiment
with this program by changing the numbers in lines 110 and
120.

The next program uses the same variable for both the X
value and the Y value in the HPLOT statement to produce a
traditional 'curve stitching' effect.

```
100 HGR
110 HCOLOR=7
120 FOR ALNG=0 TO 159 STEP 3
130     HPLOT ALNG,159 TO 0,ALNG
140 NEXT ALNG
```

It is possible to produce different effects by changing the
color at line 110 and also by varying the STEP value in
line 120.

Let us finish the lesson by using <u>two</u> variables in a FOR
loop to draw a colored triangle on the screen.

```
100 HGR                    ..... turn on
                                 graphics
110 HCOLOR=1               ..... set color
120 LNGTH=1                ..... line length
130 FOR ROW=60 TO 120      ..... count
140     HPLOT 100,ROW TO
        100+LNGTH,ROW      ..... plot a line
150     LNGTH=LNGTH+1      ..... increase length
160 NEXT ROW               ..... do it again
```

At line 140 the lines which form the triangle are drawn,
and then at line 150 the length of the line is increased.
Notice that we cannot use the variable name LENGTH because
it contains the reserved APPLESOFT function LEN.

. . . .

Exercises

(a) Change the triangle drawing program so that it can be drawn anywhere on the screen.

(b) Draw a house with blue walls and a red roof.

(c) Add a black door and two windows to the house.

(d) Draw each of the following patterns:

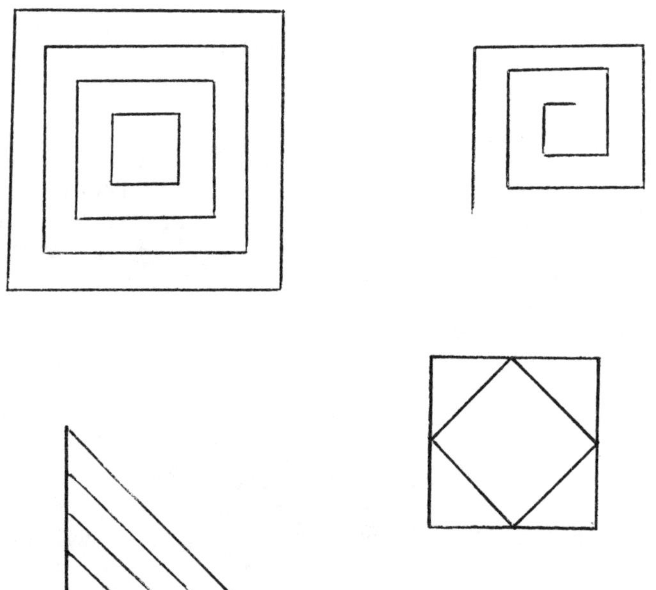

(d) Adapt the program which draws the square to draw a checker (draughts, chess) board on the screen.

(e) Produce your own 'curve stitching' pattern.

. . . .

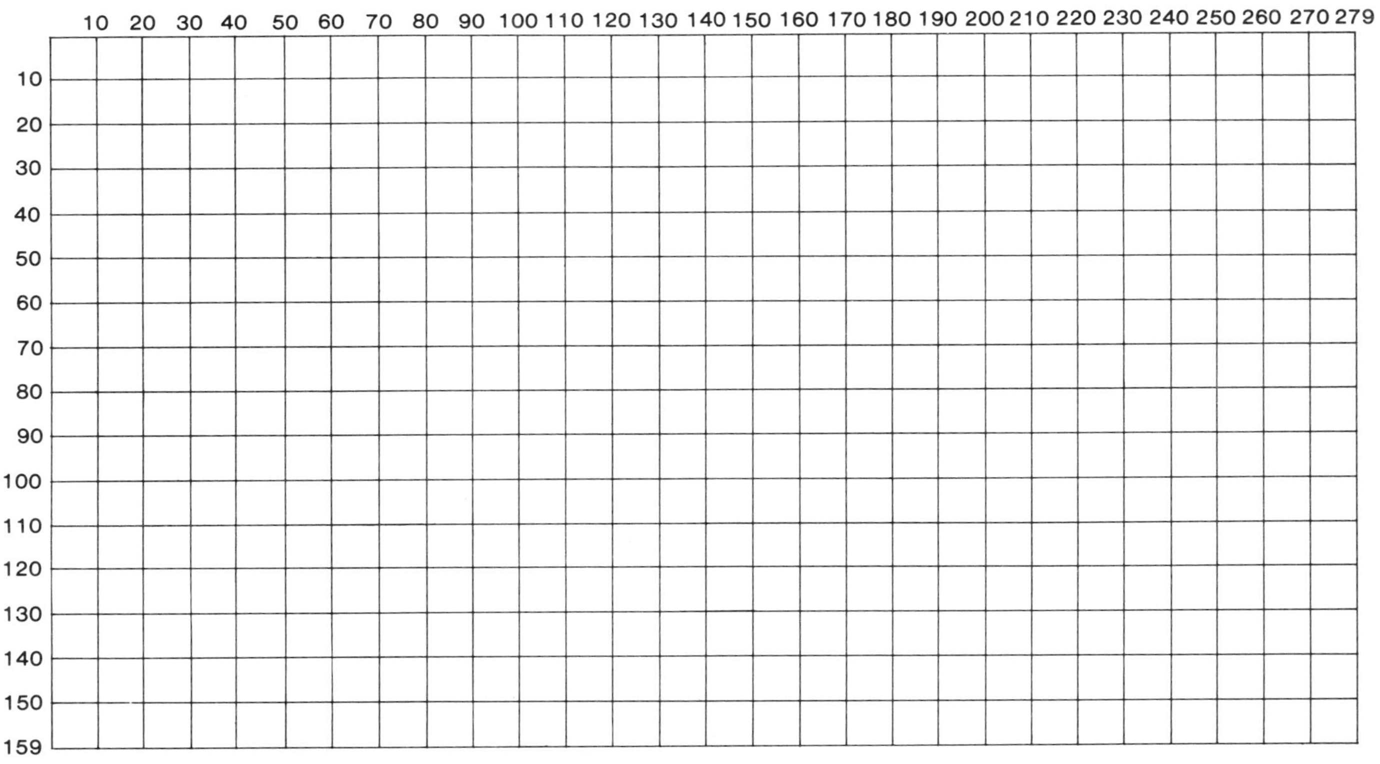

HIGH - RESOLUTION PLANNING SHEET

Interlude 2

1. The FOR loop can be extended through the use of the
   STEP command.   The STEP command is used whenever you
   wish to count by numbers other than 1.

   For example:

        FOR I=2 TO 10 STEP 2 : NEXT

   would cause the variable I to take the values 2,4,6,8
   and 10.

   The statement:

        FOR I=5 TO 1 STEP -1 : NEXT

   would cause the variable I to take the values
   5,4,3,2,1.

   Further, the statement:

        FOR I=1 TO 2 STEP 0.3 : NEXT

   would cause the variable I to take the values 1,1.3,
   1.6,1.9 and 2.2.

2. If you wish to check the values that certain variables
   are taking (especially when a program is giving
   unexpected results), the commands STOP and CONT can be
   used.   Consider the following program:

```
10 I=5 : J=3
20 I=I+1 : J=J+6
30 STOP
40 GOTO 20
```

   When the program is RUN it will STOP at line 30.   The
   user can then type:

   PRINT I,J

   6   9

   to inspect the value of those variables.   Type CONT
   and it will again STOP at line 30 where I and J will
   have the values 7 and 15.   This process can be
   continued until errors are tracked down.

3. So far we have used assignment statements to put values into memory cells.   There are two other methods of doing this known as the READ statement and the INPUT statement.   To illustrate these statements we shall analyze a program which simply counts up to a given value.

First study the following program:

```
10 READ N
20 FOR I=1 TO N
30      PRINT I
40 NEXT I
50 DATA 12
```

When the READ statement is encountered a DATA statement is searched for.   The next value found on the DATA line is assigned to the variable in the READ line.   In this case the value 12 is placed in the cell labelled N.   The numbers 1 to 12 will be printed out.   If the number on the DATA line is changed to 8,say, then the numbers 1 to 8 will be printed out.

Now consider the next program:

```
10 FOR I=1 TO 3
20      READ A,B
30      PRINT A,B
40 NEXT I
50 DATA 4,0.3,2,1.2,17,1
```

In this case the READ statement will firstly assign the value 4 to the memory cell A then 0.3 to the cell B.   Next time round the loop it will assign 2 to the cell A then 1.2 to the cell B, and so on.   Note that in this case the number of DATA items to be read is known beforehand.

Another technique is to use a TERMINATOR to signal the end of the data if the number of items can vary.   A terminator is a data item which is added to the list in order to 'terminate' or end a loop.   In the next program the aim is to add the positive numbers in the data list.   The value -1 is added to the list as a terminator.

```
10 READ N
20 IF N=-1 THEN 50
30 T=T+N
40 GOTO 10
50 PRINT T
60 END
70 DATA 4,6,8,1,6,3,-1
```

4. Sometimes the user does not know what value is
    required until it is time to run the program. Under
    these circumstances the INPUT is used to allow the
    user to type a value in while the program is running.

```
10 INPUT "NUMBER OF STUDENTS" ; N
20 FOR I=1 TO N
30 ...........
```

In this example the message

NUMBER OF STUDENTS?

will be displayed on the screen and the user then
types in a number which will be assigned to the cell
labelled N.

Lesson 3

The Text Display

In this lesson the use of the text display is explored. Techniques for highlighting text are introduced and the features of the PRINT command are explained.

The first two lessons have concentrated on the graphics
displays. This lesson will explore the features of the
text display. If the Apple is in graphics mode type:

TEXT

to return to the text display. This display consists of 24
rows of text, each with 40 characters in a row.

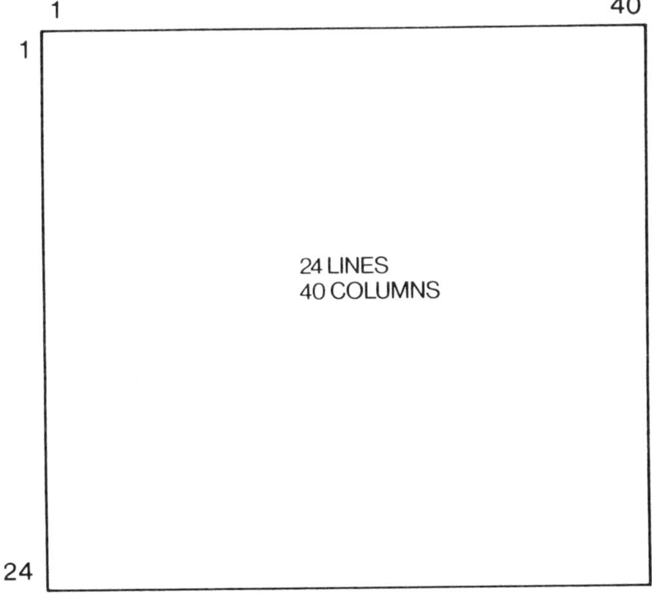

TEXT DISPLAY

The current position on the text display is indicated by a flashing CURSOR. The cursor can be controlled by a number of commands. These include:

HOME   .....   clears the text display and places the
                        cursor in the top left hand corner of
                        the screen.

HTAB X   .....   moves the cursor across to column X.

VTAB Y   .....   moves the cursor to row Y.

It is important to realize that the columns are numbered 1 to 40 and the rows are numbered 1 to 24.

To see the effect of these commands try the following program:

```
10 HOME              ..... clear the screen
20 VTAB 12           ..... move down to line 12
30 HTAB 20           ..... move across to column 20
40 PRINT "BOO"       ..... display the word BOO
```

The word BOO will be displayed in the center of the screen. It was displayed through the use of the PRINT statement. This statement will be discussed in more detail later in the lesson. The VTAB and HTAB commands can be used to make the output more appealing. For example, try the following program:

```
10 HOME                  ..... clear the screen
20 FOR I=1 TO 24         ..... count to 24
30    VTAB I             ..... move to row I
40    HTAB I             ..... move to column I
50    PRINT "WELCOME"    ..... print WELCOME
60 NEXT I                ..... increase I
```

The word "WELCOME" is printed diagonally down the screen since the values taken by the HTAB and VTAB commands increase each time around the loop. These functions are particularly useful when producing "stopwatch" displays. For example, if we wish to "see" the computer counting, the following program could be used:

```
10 HOME                    ..... clear the screen
20 VTAB 12:HTAB 16         ..... move to center of
                                 screen
30 PRINT "COUNTING"        ..... print COUNTING
40 FOR I=1 TO 100          ..... count to 100
50    VTAB 12:HTAB 26      ..... position to print I
60    PRINT I              ..... print value of I
70 NEXT I                  ..... increase I
80 END
```

You will see that the numbers flash up very quickly. To
slow the program down, insert the following line:

```
55 FOR J=1 TO 50 : NEXT J
```

Displays can be further enhanced with the use of the
NORMAL, INVERSE and FLASH commands.   These have the
following effect:

NORMAL   ..... restore normal white on black output.

INVERSE   ..... all subsequent output will be displayed
                      as black on white.

FLASH   ..... all subsequent output to the screen will
                      be flashing.

Note that these commands only affect the output, anything
typed from the keyboard will not be affected.   Try the
following program:


```
10 HOME
20 VTAB 12 : HTAB 20
30 INVERSE
40 PRINT "PLEASE WAIT"
50 NORMAL
60 END
```


You will notice that the message PLEASE WAIT is printed as
black-on-white rather than white-on-black.   Line 50 is
essential for restoring normal output. To draw attention
to a message even more dramatically, substitute the command
FLASH for INVERSE at line 30.

. . . .

Exercises

(a) Clear the screen, then display the word APPLE at the
     top of the screen.

(b) Clear the screen, then display the word APPLE in the
     bottom right hand corner of the screen.

(c) Adapt the WELCOME program so that the numbers 1 to 20
     are displayed diagonally across the screen.

(d) Use the STEP command in a FOR...NEXT loop to produce a
     COUNTDOWN display.

(e) Write a program which displays the word BOO down the
     center of the screen twenty times. The first ten
     times the word should be in inverse video, the next
     ten times the word should be flashing.

. . . .

Let us now develop a program which will print the time in
hours, minutes and seconds. The time will be displayed in
row 12 on the screen.

```
10  HOME : SECS=0 : MINS=0 : HRS=0
20  VTAB 12 : HTAB 10
30  INVERSE : PRINT "HOURS";
40  HTAB 20 : PRINT "MINS";
50  HTAB 29 : PRINT "SECS";
60     SECS=SECS+1
70     IF SECS=60 THEN HTAB 26 : PRINT "   "; :
       SECS=0 : MINS=MINS+1
80     IF MINS=60 THEN HTAB 17 : PRINT "   "; :
       MINS=0 : HRS=HRS+1
90     FOR PAUSE=1 TO 665 : NEXT PAUSE
100    NORMAL
110    HTAB 8 : PRINT HRS;
120    HTAB 17 : PRINT MINS;
130    HTAB 26 : PRINT SECS;
140 GOTO 60
```

This program will continue indefinitely. This is
controlled by the loop which has been created by the GOTO
statement at line 140.   The "body" of the loop has been

indented so that it can be identified more clearly. Note
that at lines 70 and 80 a check must be made to see if the
number of minutes or seconds has reached 60. If either of
these conditions has been met then the display must be
cleared (by printing two spaces) and the variable reset.
You may wish to change the final value in the PAUSE loop in
line 90.   The value of 665 has been chosen as an
approximate delay of one second. A more exact value could
be found by constantly checking the program against a stop
watch.   The use of the semi-colons after the PRINT
statements will be explained shortly.

The PRINT statement has already been introduced. It is one
of the most important statements in the APPLESOFT language,
since it is through this statement that the results of
programs are communicated to the user.   It is highly
desirable that the full features of the PRINT statement and
its associated functions are used to ensure that output is
readable and easy to understand.

Some further features of this statement are:

***   it is used to display information on the text screen,
       or at the bottom of the graphics screen.

***   it can be used to display the value of variables.

           10 A=1 : B=2.2
           20 PRINT A,B

           RUN
           1   2.2

***   any text enclosed in inverted commas will be displayed
       "as is" on the screen.

           10 PRINT "THE CAT SAT ON THE MAT"

           RUN
           THE CAT SAT ON THE MAT

***   variables or text strings can be separated by either
       commas or semi-colons. Commas are used to separate
       data into columns which are 14 characters wide.
       Semi-colons are used to compress output.

***   the following program shows the difference between the
       comma and the semi-colon.

```
10 A=1 : B=2
20 PRINT A,B
30 PRINT A;B
40 PRINT "THE VALUE OF A IS",A
50 PRINT "THE VALUE OF B IS";B

RUN
1                   2
12
THE VALUE OF A IS                1
THE VALUE OF B IS2
```

*** finishing a PRINT statement with a semi-colon ensures
     that the output from the next PRINT statement will
     continue from that place on the screen.

```
10 PRINT "HOW ";
20 PRINT "ARE ";
30 PRINT "YOU"

RUN
HOW ARE YOU
```

*** any expression in a PRINT statement will be evaluated.

```
10 COST=20
20 PRINT "THE TAX ON $";COST;" IS $";.15*COST

RUN
THE TAX ON $20 IS $3
```

*** text can be "scrolled" using the PRINT command. The
     following code would scroll the text up five lines.

```
FOR I=1 TO 5 : PRINT : NEXT I
```

PRINT statements can be used in conjunction with the
special functions SPC and TAB. The TAB function moves the
cursor across the row to the printing position which is
specified in brackets. TAB(10), for example, moves the
cursor to column 10 and TAB(35) moves the cursor to column
35.   If the cursor has already passed the specified
position, it does not move. The SPC function moves the
cursor across a number of spaces regardless of its current
position. Run the following programs to see the difference
between the two functions.

```
10 FOR I=6 TO 15
20    PRINT I;TAB(10);I
30 NEXT I
```

and

```
10 FOR I=6 TO 15
20    PRINT I;SPC(10);I
30 NEXT I
```

The SPC function, when combined with the INVERSE command,
can produce some very interesting effects. Compare the
effects of the following programs:

```
50 HOME
100 FOR I=1 TO 11
150    PRINT SPC(40)
200 NEXT I
250 VTAB 6 : HTAB 16 : PRINT "MY PROGRAM"
```

and

```
50  HOME : INVERSE
100 FOR I=1 TO 11
150    PRINT SPC(40)
200 NEXT I
250 VTAB 6 : HTAB 16 : NORMAL
300 PRINT "MY PROGRAM"
```

This effect can be used to produce interesting displays at
the beginning and the end of programs.

The SPC function can also be used to erase text which is
already on the screen. Consider the following program:

```
10 HOME                       ..... clear the
                                     screen
20 VTAB 10 : HTAB 12          ..... move down &
                                     across
30 PRINT "BALL";              ..... print BALL
40 FOR PAUSE=1 TO 200:NEXT    ..... wait a while
50 HTAB 12 : PRINT SPC(4)     ..... wipe it out
```

This idea can be used to "play" with words on the screen.
The following program is similar to the "ball-bouncing"
program in lesson 1. In this case the word BALL will
bounce up and down.

```
 10 HOME
 20 ROW=15
 30 DIR=1
 40    VTAB ROW : HTAB 18
 50    PRINT "BALL";
 60    ROW=ROW+DIR
 70    FOR PAUSE=1 TO 200:NEXT
 80    HTAB 18 : PRINT SPC(4);
 90    IF ROW=24 OR ROW=15 THEN DIR=-DIR
100 GOTO 40
```

The variable ROW indicates the current row in which the
word BALL is being printed, and the variable DIR is used to
indicate the direction the ball is travelling in. When the
ball is moving down, DIR has a value of 1; when the ball is
moving up, DIR has a value of -1.

. . . .

Exercises

(a) Use a PRINT statement and a FOR loop to display the
     two times table.

     HINT: use a TAB function.

(b) A shopkeeper requires a list which shows what the
     sales tax of 27% would be for all his goods. If his
     goods cost even dollar amounts from $2 to $40 print a
     table (with headings) showing the value of the item,
     then the sales tax and the total cost.

(c) Using the bouncing ball program as a model, produce
     the following effects:

     (i)   make the word PLANE "fly" across the screen;

     (ii) make the word ELEVATOR stop at four "floors" as
           it moves up the screen;

     (iii) make a PLANE drop a BOMB;

     (iv) make a CATERPILLAR crawl across the screen;

     (v)   make a CAR accelerate across the screen.

     (vi) make up your own effect.

(d)   Print the flashing message:

                WARNING !!

                COMPUTER IN USE!!

      on the screen.

(e)   Print the numbers 1 to 12 across the screen with one
      space between each number.

(f)   A data list contains fifteen code numbers of products
      as well as the number of each which is in stock.
      Print out the code numbers and the number in stock in
      columns under suitable headings.

              CODE NUMBER   NO IN STOCK
              ***********   ***********
                 3104   24
                 7120   34
      etc.

(g)   One way of printing large letters on the screen is to
      "code" them on DATA lines. Thus the letter E would
      look like this:

      ****
      *
      **
      *
      ****

      and would be coded as:

      DATA 4,1,2,1,4

      since the numbers represent the number of asterisks on
      each line. Write a program which will display a
      letter of your choice. For many letters you will need
      to print a number of spaces before the asterisk. How
      could this be coded?

. . . .

Interlude 3

The Applesoft language incorporates a number of mathematics functions which are very useful.   The functions are :

ABS ATN COS EXP INT LOG RND TAN SGN SIN SQR

three of these will be discussed here.

RND

This function generates a random number which is greater than or equal to 0 and less than 1.   The result can be assigned to a variable :

        Y = RND(1)

or printed directly

        PRINT RND(1)

or used in an expression

        NMBR = 10 * RND(1) + 1

If the function RND(X) is used then the value of X is important.   If X is negative then the same sequence of random numbers is generated each time that value of X is used.   If X is zero then the most recent random number is generated.   If X is positive then a new random number is produced each time.   Try the following program a number of times and examine the output carefully.

```
100 INPUT "ENTER -1,0 OR 1" ; X
110 FOR I = 1 TO 10
120     PRINT RND(X)
130 NEXT I
140 END
```

Notice that nearly all the numbers contain a decimal part. Very few whole numbers (integers) are generated.   If we wish to randomly produce whole numbers (e.g. for dice tossing), a new function must be introduced.

INT

The INT function returns the largest integer which is less than or equal to the number.   Examine the following table to see how it works :

X	INT (X)
2.5	2
2.999	2
2.01	2
2	2
1.999	1
0	0
-0.5	-1
-2	-2
-2.1	-3

This function can be used in conjunction with the RND function to produce whole numbers.   For example the following program will produce 10 random whole numbers :

```
100 FOR I = 1 TO 10
110     PRINT INT(10* RND(1))
120 NEXT I
```

Run the program a few times.   Notice that the largest number produced is 9 and the smallest number is 0.   If we wished to generate the numbers on a dice then the random number must be multiplied first by 6.   This will produce whole numbers in the range 0 to 5.   To change this to the range 1 to 6 simply add 1.

```
PRINT INT(6 * RND(1) + 1)
```

In general the formula

```
INT(B * RND(1) + A)
```

can be used to produce random numbers in the range $A <= X < A+B$.

Another use of the INT function is to check if one number is divisible by another.   Study the following code :

```
100 FOR I = 1 TO 5
110     IF I/2 = INT(I/2) THEN PRINT I
120 NEXT I
```

```
RUN
2
4
```

Notice that the even numbers (i.e. those divisible by 2)
were output.   To check if a number is divisible by N use:

        IF I/N = INT(I/N) THEN ......

ABS

The ABS function returns the ABSolute value of an
expression.   If the number is positive or zero it remains
unchanged.   If the number is negative then the positive
value of the number is returned.

X	ABS(X)
1	1
1.6	1.6
0.001	0.001
0	0
-2	2
-0.01	0.01

The following line of code checks to see if the value of X
is close to the value of Y.

        IF ABS(X-Y) <0.01 THEN PRINT "CLOSE"

Lesson 4

String Handling

This lesson introduces methods for manipulating text. As one of the most common applications of this idea is in word processing, some of the examples have been chosen to give a simple insight into this field.

Up until this lesson only numbers have been assigned to
memory cells.   It is also possible to put "strings" of
letters and other characters into memory cells.   The term
STRING refers to any collection of characters which is
produced by a computer.   The Apple uses the $ symbol to
distinguish between cells which store numbers and cells
which store STRINGS.   Consider this program:

```
10   A$ = "FRED"
20   PRINT A$
RUN
FRED
```

In this example the string FRED is assigned to the cell
labelled A$, then printed out.   Note that the string to be
assigned must be enclosed in inverted commas.   One use for
this idea is in answering questions such as:

DO YOU WISH TO PLAY AGAIN?

or

ANOTHER NUMBER?

This can be done by using the following code:

```
200   INPUT "DO YOU ---- AGAIN"; A$
210   IF A$ = "YES" THEN 10
```

The same idea can be used to allow the computer to print
out a person's name in a tutorial.

```
1000   INPUT "HELLO, WHAT IS YOUR NAME" ; N$
1100   PRINT "NICE TO MEET YOU" ; N$
1200   PRINT "HERE ARE SOME QUESTIONS"

RUN
HELLO, WHAT IS YOUR NAME? JILL
NICE TO MEET YOU JILL
HERE ARE SOME QUESTIONS
```

In this example the user types in her name in response to
the question.   The name is then stored in the cell
labelled N$ and can then be used elsewhere in the program.

Strings can also be stored on DATA lines then READ into
string variables.   The following program prints a simple
invoice.   The DATA lines hold the name of the article
bought, the number bought and the unit cost.

```
 800    HOME
1000    FOR I = 1 TO 5
1100        READ ITEM$, NO, UCOST
1200        SUBTL = NO * UCOST
1300        PRINT ITEM$;TAB(12);NO;TAB(20);UCOST;
            TAB(28);SUBTL
1400        TTL = TTL + SUBTL
1500    NEXT I
1600    PRINT TAB(29);"****"
1700    PRINT TAB(29);"$";TTL
1800    PRINT TAB(29);"****"

9999    END
10000   DATA HAMMER   , 5 ,   3.00
10100   DATA SAW      , 2 ,   5.00
10300   DATA SHOVEL   , 3 ,  14.00
10400   DATA HOSE     , 1 ,  12.00
10500   DATA CHISEL   , 3 ,   3.00
```

Add some extra code to this program so that each of the columns has a heading.

String functions can be joined together with the + sign; this process is known as CONCATENATION.   This process simply joins one string to the end of another.   Study the following program.

```
1000    INPUT "GIVEN NAME? "; G$
1100    INPUT "SURNAME? " ; S$
1200    N$ = G$ + S$
1300    PRINT "YOUR NAME IS " ; N$

RUN
GIVEN NAME? FRED
SURNAME? SMITH
YOUR NAME IS FREDSMITH
```

Notice that the strings have been joined together as requested, but there is no space between the given name and the surname.   To overcome this problem try the following:

```
1000    INPUT "GIVEN NAME? " ; G$
1100    INPUT "SURNAME? " ; S$
1200    N$ = G$ + " " + S$
1300    PRINT "YOUR NAME IS " ; N$
```

This has the effect of adding a space (which is also a string) between the surname and the given name.   Another example of this process is given in the following program in which three questions are asked so that a DATE string can be formed.

```
1000   INPUT "MONTH? "  ; M$
1100   INPUT "DAY? "    ; D$
1200   INPUT "YEAR? "   ; Y$
1300   DTE$ = M$ + "-" + D$ + "-" + Y$
1400   PRINT "THE DATE IS " ; DTE$

RUN
MONTH? DECEMBER
DAY  ? 23
YEAR ? 1982
THE DATE IS DECEMBER-23-1982
```

One problem with this program is that it allows a wide variety of alternatives, for example, D, DEC, DECEM, DECEMBER, etc. for each of the responses.   An elementary method of overcoming this problem is provided by the LEN function.   This function returns a NUMBER which represents the number of characters in the string.   The following table shows some of the values of LEN(A$):

A$	LEN(A$)	
**	*******	
CAT	3	
FRED SMITH	10	count the space
ABC123*?	8	
A. B. C. D.	11	three spaces

We can therefore use this function to restrict input to three characters for the month, two for the day and four for the year.   Remember the symbol <> means NOT EQUAL.

```
1000   INPUT "MONTH? "  ; M$
1100   IF LEN(M$) <> 3 THEN PRINT "ERROR" : GOTO
       1000
1200   INPUT "DAY? " ; D$
1300   IF LEN (D$) <>2 THEN PRINT "ERROR" : GOTO
       1200
1400   INPUT "YEAR? " ; Y$
1500   IF LEN(Y$) <> 4 THEN PRINT "ERROR" : GOTO
       1400
1600   DTE$ = M$ + "-" + D$ + "-" + Y$
1700   PRINT DTE$
```

Note that we have just carried out a process known as
VALIDATION. We have performed a simple check on the input
data. Just because each check was passed, however, does
not mean that the data are correct. The date XXX-DD-17Y3,
however, would have passed the tests in this program.

The LEN function is widely used in STRING handling. One
of the areas in which it is widely used is WORD PROCESSING.
We shall look at one simple example. Imagine that we were
writing a report and wished to have a cover page which
looked like this:

                        A REPORT

                           TO

                          THE

                   MANAGING DIRECTOR

One way of doing this would be through a series of PRINT
statements in which you laboriously worked out how to
center each of the statements.   A simpler alternative
would be to use the LEN function and the INT function
(introduced in the last interlude) to automatically center
each of the headings.

```
    800   HOME
   1000   FOR I = 1 TO 4
   1100      READ A$
   1200      L=LEN(A$)
   1300      PSTN = INT ((40-L)/2)
   1400      VTAB I*4
   1500      PRINT TAB(PSTN); A$
   1600   NEXT I
   9999   END
  10000   DATA A REPORT
  10100   DATA TO , THE
  10200   DATA MANAGING DIRECTOR
```

At line 1200 the length of each statement is calculated,
then at line 1300 the number of spaces to TAB is worked out
using a simple formula. Substitute your own message in
the DATA lines.

· ·

Exercises

(a)   A DATA list contains the name of each employee and his
      or her annual salary.   Write a program which will
      read in each employee and salary and print out his or
      her weekly pay.

(b)   Use concatenation plus the text centering routine to
      fill the screen with the following display:

```
                    A
                   AAA
                  AAAAA
                 AAAAAAA
```

      If A$ is the string to be centered a statement such as

```
          A$ = A$ + "AA"
```

      may help to produce the pattern.

(c)   A DATA list contains the names of 5 Social Science
      teachers.   They are to be assigned to classes 1 to 5
      according to their order in the list.   Write a
      program which will print a label for each teacher.

      e.g.

```
          MISS P. SMITH
          SOCIAL SCIENCE
          CLASSROOM 1
```

· ·

The LEN function has already been introduced.   There are a
number of other functions which allow the user to
manipulate strings.   The most important of these are the
LEFT$, RIGHT$ and MID$ functions.   Note that each of these
functions returns a STRING not a number.

Study each of the following models carefully. Some programs
will be developed which use them to manipulate text.

. . . .

MODEL 9

The LEFT function is used to extract the LEFT part of a
string. The structure is:

        LEFT$(APPLE$,N)

this would extract the LEFT N characters from the string
APPLE$. Thus LEFT$(APPLE$,3) would extract the string APP.

. . . .

MODEL 10

The RIGHT function is used to extract the RIGHT part of a
string. The structure is:

        RIGHT$(APPLE$,N)

this would extract the RIGHT N characters from the string
APPLE$.   Thus RIGHT$(APPLE$,3) would extract the string
PLE.

. . . .

MODEL 11

The MID function is used to extract the MIDdle part of a string. The structure is:

                MID$(APPLE$,M,N)

this would extract the MIDdle N characters starting from character M.   Thus MID$(APPLE$,3,2) would extract the string PL.

Study the output from the following programs.   They give examples of the use of each function:

```
1000   A$ = "TASMANIA"
1100   FOR I = 1 TO LEN(A$)
1200       PRINT LEFT$(A$,I)
1300   NEXT I
```

Note that at line 1100 the LEN function is used to calculate the length of the string A$.

```
1000   A$ = "TASMANIA"
1100   FOR I = 1 TO LEN(A$)
1200       PRINT RIGHT$(A$,I)
1300   NEXT I
```

The MID function can be used to extract strings from within other strings.   The following program "breaks" a sentence up into single letters.

```
1000   S$ = "THE CAT SAT ON THE MAT"
1100   FOR I = 1 TO LEN(S$)
1200      PRINT MID$(S$,I,1)
1300   NEXT I
```

Each letter will be displayed down the screen.   It takes
only a minor variation of this program to print each word
separately.

```
1000   S$ = "THE CAT SAT ON THE MAT"
1100   FOR I = 1 TO LEN(S$)
1200      L$ = MID$ (S$,I,1)
1300       IF L$ = " " THEN PRINT : GOTO 1500
1400       PRINT L$;
1500   NEXT I
RUN
THE
CAT
SAT
ON
THE
MAT
```

At line 1200 each character is extracted.   Line 1300 is
used to check if the character is a space - if it is, then
the space is not printed and the cursor is moved to the
next line.

The next program searches for the occurrence of one string
inside another.   The MID function is used to search for
the string; therefore we have to ensure that the search
stops <u>before</u> the end of the string is reached.

```
1000   T$="THE CAT SAT ON THE MAT"      ..... string to search
1100    INPUT "SEARCH STRING";S$        ..... string to search
                                              for
1200    S=LEN(S$)                       ..... length of search
                                              string
1300    PSTN=0                          ..... string found here
1400    ND=LEN(T$)-S+1                   ..... stop search here
1500    FOR I = 1 TO ND
1600       IF MID$(T$,I,S)=S$ THEN      ..... found?
              PSTN=I : I=ND             ..... note where found
1700    NEXT I
1800    IF PSTN=0 THEN PRINT
        "STRING NOT FOUND"
1900    IF PSTN <> 0 THEN PRINT
        "STRING FOUND AT POSTION ";PSTN
9999    END
```

If the search string is found, the loop counter is set to the last value, so that an orderly exit from the loop is executed.   Note that the variable PSTN is used to note the position of the search string.

Another function which is very useful is the VAL function which converts strings into numbers if it is possible. Note that the VAL function returns a NUMBER not a string.

```
1000   A$= "ABC123XYZ"      ..... assign a string to A$
1100   B$= MID$(A$,4,3)     ..... assign 123 to B$
1200   B = VAL(B$)          ..... convert it to a number
1300   PRINT B*2            ..... output result

RUN
246
```

Two other important functions enable the user to take advantage of the internal coding system used by the Apple. The Apple uses the ASCII code (American Standard Code for Information Interchange) to represent all characters. These codes are given in Appendix C.   As soon as a character is typed on the keyboard, the Apple converts it to the corresponding ASCII code.   For example, A is represented by the number 65, the digit 5 is represented by the number 53 and a space is represented by 32.   The function ASC returns the ASCII code of a character and the function CHR$ converts an ASCII code to a character.   An important use of these functions is to check input data. If the response to a question must be a letter, for example, then the following code could be used as a check:

```
1000   INPUT "TYPE A LETTER " ; L$
1100   IF ASC(L$)< 65 OR ASC(L$)>90 THEN
            PRINT "NOT A LETTER" : GOTO 1000
1200   PRINT "THANK YOU"
```

The following program "codes" a message by subtracting 10 from the ASCII value of each character:

```
1000   INPUT "MESSAGE:" ; M$
1100   PRINT "CODED MESSAGE: ";
1200   FOR I = 1 TO LEN(M$)
1300       C$ = MID$(M$,I,1)
1400       C=ASC(C$)
1500       C=C-10
1600       C$=CHR$(C)
1700       PRINT C$;
1800   NEXT I
```

The following program stores the alphabet in the cell A$.

```
1000   A$=""
1100   FOR I=65 TO 90
1200       A$=A$ + CHR$(I)
1300   NEXT I
1400   PRINT A$
```

The final program in this lesson uses most of the functions introduced in this chapter to produce a very simple simulation of "word wrapping" which is commonly used in word processing. Word processing operators do not want to check when they have reached the end of a line in order to press the RETURN key, and they do not want to have words broken across lines. This program checks to see if the text is over 30 characters wide and if it is the last word is taken from the current line and placed on the next line. The GET statement used at line 1100 causes any character typed to be assigned directly to the variable L$ <u>without</u> RETURN being pressed.

```
1000   HOME : LYNE=1
1100   GET L$ : IF L$ = CHR$(27) THEN 9999
1150   PRINT L$; : LN$ = LN$ + L$
1200   IF LEN(LN$) <30 THEN 1100
1300   FOR J=30 TO 1 STEP-1
1400       IF MID$(LN$,J,1)=CHR$(32)THEN 1700
1500   NEXT J
1600   PRINT "ERROR" : GOTO 9999
1700   VTAB LYNE:HTAB1:PRINT SPC(40):VTAB LYNE
1800   PRINT LEFT$(LN$,J):L=LEN(LN$)
1900   LYNE=LYNE+1 : LN$=RIGHT$(LN$,L-J):PRINT LN$;
2000   GOTO 1100
9999   END
```

The explanation of this program is as follows:
LINE 1000 : the screen is cleared and a line counter is set
            to 1
LINE 1100 : a character is typed at the keyboard.   The IF
            statement checks to see if the ESC key has been
            pressed.
LINE 1150 : the character is typed on the screen.   The
            current line is stored in LN$.
LINE 1200 : this line checks to see if the line is longer
            than 30 characters.
LINE 1300 : if the line is longer, then the FOR loop scans
            back along the line until a space is found.
LINE 1400 : a character in the line is checked to see if it
            is a space (CHR$32).

LINE 1500 : continue the loop
LINE 1600 : no spaces in the line - the program gives up.
LINE 1700 : the current line is wiped out
LINE 1800 : the text up to the last word is reprinted.
LINE 1900 : the last word is now stored in LN$ and is
            printed on the next line.
LINE 2000 : do it all again.

The program is a very simple simulation which will not work
under all conditions. However, it does provide a practical
example of the use of many of the functions discussed in
this chapter.

. . . .

Exercises

(a)   In each of the following exercises imagine that a
        date is input in the form MMM-DD-YY (e.g. MAR-05-81
        or DEC-25-82).

        Write a program to input a date then print out the
        month.

(b)   Write a program to input a date then print out the
        day.

(c)   Write a program to input a date then print out the
        year in the form 19YY.

(d)   Input a date then print the message DAY VALID if the
        day is in the range 1 to 31, otherwise print the
        message DAY INVALID.

(e)   Input a date then check to see if it is the correct
        length (i.e. 9 characters).

(f)   Input a date in the form MMM-DD-YY then print it out
        in the form MMM-DD-19YY.

(g)   The following section of code accepts the number of
        a month then prints out the name of that month

```
1000 MNTH$="JAN FEB MAR APR MAY JUN JUL AUG SEP OCT
          NOV DEC"
1100 INPUT "MONTH NUMBER " ; N
1200 M$ = MID$(MNTH$, 4*N-3,3)
1300 PRINT M$
```

Use the same concept to check if the day given is valid for a particular month. Store the maximum number of days in a similar string:

NDS=" 31 29 31 30 31 30 31 31 30 31 30 31"

(h)   Write a program to input today's date and a person's birthdate then print out the person's age in years, months and days.

(i)   Assign the string ***** to the cell STAR$ then output the following pattern.

        *
        * *
        * * *
        * * * *
        * * * * *

(j)   Write a program which counts the number of words in a sentence.

(k)   Books are identified by a code known as an ISBN. Since these numbers are very long it is possible for errors to occur when the number is typed into a computer. To overcome this the last digit is known as a CHECK DIGIT, and is calculated from the other digits. Study the following example :

              ISBN NO   0 224 00960 5

              0 X 1 =   0
              2 X 2 =   4
              2 X 3 =   6
              4 X 4 = 16
              0 X 5 =   0
              0 X 6 =   0
              9 X 7 = 63
              6 X 8 = 48
              0 X 9 =   0
                         ____
                          137
                         ____

Remainder when 137 is divided by 11 = 5

Notice that this is the same as the last digit in the ISBN.

Use this method to write a program which accepts an
ISBN then checks to see if it is valid.

(l)   Write a program which accepts money amounts in
        number form then prints out the amount in words.

(m)   Tasmanian license plates consist of two letters
        followed by four digits (e.g. AB 1463, XY 4073).
        Imagine that the plates are to be printed by
        computer and that the license number is to be stored
        in a string variable.   If the manufacturer starts
        at number AA 0001 and continues to ZZ 9999, write a
        program which will automatically generate the next
        number.

. . . .

Interlude 4

By now you will have noticed that some of the programs are becoming quite long and hard to read.   This brings us to one of the most important things you need to learn in programming - programming style!   The longer a program is, the more vital it is to properly document the program. This not only makes it easier for someone else to follow the program, it also helps the author to track down mistakes.

One of the important statements to use when setting out programs neatly is the REM (for REMark) statement.   BASIC does not try to process anything after a REM statement therefore we can write comments on those lines.   Consider the following program:

```
100    REM
150    REM   MY FAVOURITE PROGRAM
200    REM
250    REM   WRITTEN BY BILL SMITH
300    REM
```

If you now type:

RUN

nothing will be printed out.   This is because every line in the program contains a REM statement hence the whole program consists of comments.   If similar statements were included at the beginning of a program, however, it would become a "TITLE" which would identify who wrote it.   An additional method of setting out remarks is through the use of the colon as a statement separator.   If a line number is followed by a colon and nothing else, the line number will be retained in the code.   This helps to separate sections of code from one another.

```
100 :
150 :
200 REM PAYROLL PROGRAM
250 :
300 :
350 REM WRITTEN BY B. SMITH
400 :
450 :
```

Notice that this can make the code easier to read.   Now consider a program which draws a square on the high resolution screen.

```
100    REM
150    REM   DISPLAY A SQUARE
200    REM
500    REM   INITIALIZE VARIABLES
520    SIDE = 40   :   REM length of side
540    X = 20   : REM X-value of corner
560    Y = 60   : REM Y-value of corner
800    REM OTHER INITIALIZATION
820    HGR   :   REM turn on graphics
840    HCOLOR=7 : REM set color to white
850    :
860    :
1000       REM DRAW THE SQUARE
1100 HPLOT X,Y TO X+SIDE,Y : REM BOTTOM SIDE
1200 HPLOT X+SIDE,Y TO X+SIDE,Y+SIDE : REM RIGHT SIDE
1300 HPLOT X+SIDE,Y+SIDE TO X,Y+SIDE : REM TOP SIDE
1400 PLOT X,Y+SIDE TO X,Y              : REM LEFT SIDE
9999 END
```

Notice that REM statements were used to form the 'title' of
the program and also to comment on the use of each variable
and each line.

Lesson 5

Arrays

In this lesson very few new programming techniques are introduced, rather the idea of manipulating data in arrays is discussed. The final text analysis program may cause problems for some students.

The following section of code reads the marks gained by twenty students on a test then prints out the average mark. Note the use of the PRINT statement as a prompt. This idea can be used as a model in many similar situations.

```
1000  FOR I = 1 TO 20
1100      PRINT "MARK FOR STUDENT " ; I;
1200      INPUT M
1300      T=T+M
1400  NEXT I
1500  PRINT "AVERAGE MARK ";T/20
```

The average mark will be printed as required. What would happen, however, if we needed to know the mark for a particular student or if we wanted to print a list of below-average students?   Each time a mark is input, the previous mark in the variable M is erased.   It is obvious that a new data structure is required.   In this lesson we shall consider single dimension arrays (also known as lists or vectors).

If we use the analogy of a variable as a single motel room, a model can be developed which helps to explain the structure of arrays.

. . . .

MODEL 12

Imagine a set of motel rooms and consider the following:

    motel rooms are joined together;
    motel rooms are numbered;
    the number of people in the rooms may vary.

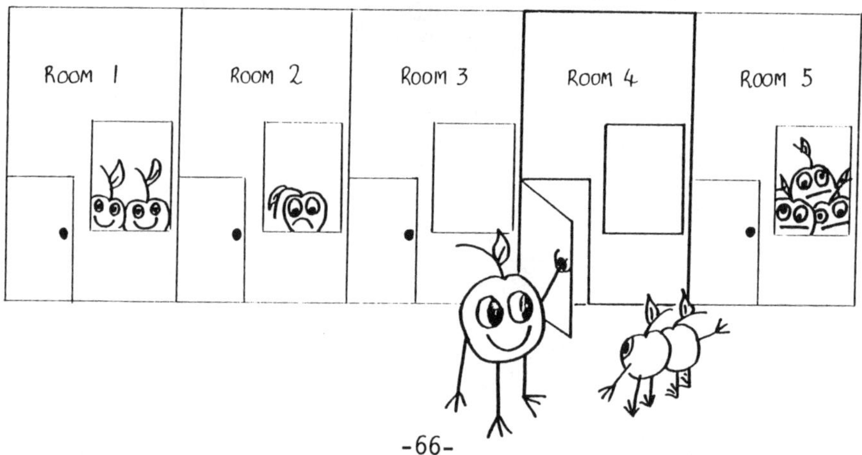

The maid might be given the following set of instructions
about cleaning the rooms:

        CLEAN Room 1
        CLEAN Room 2
        CLEAN Room 3
        CLEAN Room 4
        CLEAN Room 5

Since the rooms are related in some way the instructions
could be shortened to:

        FOR I = 1 TO 5

                CLEAN Room I

        NEXT I

If the maid wished to change her schedule she could

        FOR I = 5 TO 1 STEP -1

                CLEAN Room I

        NEXT I

This method provides a simple means of referring to a
number of similarly named objects.

. . . .

Now consider the motel to be an ARRAY of VARIABLES.   Each
variable will have the same NAME or LABEL but each will
have a different INDEX (room number).   In an Applesoft
program we also need to say how many variables (rooms) need
to be reserved (built).   To reserve a number of variables
use the statement:

        DIM ROOM(5)

This statement reserves five variables called ROOM(1),
ROOM(2), ROOM(3), ROOM(4) and ROOM(5).

The following program uses an array to store the number of
people in each room of a motel.

```
   600   DIM ROOM(5)
  1000   FOR I = 1 TO 5
  1100      READ ROOM(I)
  1200   NEXT I
 10000   DATA 2,1,0,3,1
```

After this program is RUN the array will have the following
values stored:

ROOM(1)	ROOM(2)	ROOM(3)	ROOM(4)	ROOM(5)
2	1	0	3	1

If the total number of people staying at the motel was
required then the following code could be inserted in the
previous program:

```
  1300   FOR I = 1 TO 5
  1400      T = T + ROOM(I)
  1500   NEXT I
  1600   PRINT "TOTAL= ";T
```

Notice that at line 1400 the value of the variable is
increased by the value in the array variables ROOM(1), then
ROOM(2), and so on.

These array variables can be treated in the same way as
other variables, thus if we wished to find an empty room
the following test could be applied:

```
  IF ROOM(I)=0 THEN PRINT "ROOM ";I; " IS EMPTY"
```

These ideas will now be put together in a program which
reads the number of people in each room into an array then
prints out the total and a list of empty rooms. These
instructions could have been combined into one FOR loop;
however, there are advantages in separating each process
(i.e. reading the data, calculating the total, printing the
list) into distinct MODULES.

```
 600    DIM ROOM(20)
1000    REM READ NO IN EACH ROOM
1100    FOR I = 1 TO 20
1200       READ ROOM(I)
1300    NEXT I

1400    REM CALCULATE TOTAL
1500    FOR I = 1 TO 20
1600       T = T + ROOM(I)
1700    NEXT I
1800    PRINT "TOTAL ";T

1900    REM LIST OF EMPTY ROOMS
2000    FOR I = 1 TO 20
2100       IF ROOM(I)> 0 THEN 2300
2200       PRINT "ROOM ";I;" IS EMPTY"
2300    NEXT I
9999    END
10000   REM DATA LIST
10100   DATA 2,1,0,3,1,2,2,0,3,4,1,2,1,0,1,1,2,2,1,2

RUN
TOTAL 31
ROOM 3 IS EMPTY
ROOM 8 IS EMPTY
ROOM 14 IS EMPTY
```

It is also possible to reserve string arrays.   The
following program reads in the names of the authors of a
set of books, then prints out the number of books written
by Alistair Maclean.

```
 600    DIM BOOK$(50)
1000    REM READ AUTHORS' NAMES
1100    FOR I = 1 TO 12
1200       READ BOOK$(I)
1300    NEXT I
1400    REM SCAN THE ARRAY FOR MACLEAN
1500    FOR J = 1 TO 12
1600       IF BOOK$(J)="MACLEAN" THEN N=N+1
1700    NEXT J
1800    PRINT "NO. OF BOOKS BY MACLEAN ";N
9999    END

10000   REM DATA LIST
10100   DATA MACLEAN, LUDLUM, TREVANIAN, WEST, ARCHER,
           MACLEAN, MORRELL
10200   DATA HAILEY, MACLEAN, HAILEY, TOLKEIN, URIS
```

Notice that at line 600 fifty string array variables were
reserved but only twelve were used.   This does not matter
- it is better to reserve some extra variables rather than
run out. Also notice that the second FOR loop uses the
variable J for the index whereas the first FOR loop used
the variable I.   The name of the variable does not matter
- it is the VALUE of the variable that is important.
Lines 1500 to 1700 constitute a process known as a LINEAR
SEARCH - where the contents of the array are scanned for a
particular value.

Arrays are a very common data structure and a large number
of processes are needed to deal effectively with data which
are stored in arrays.   We have already seen how to SEARCH
an array.   Other processes include finding the maximum
value in an array, finding the minimum value, sorting the
data into ascending or descending order and many more.   A
detailed study of these processes is beyond the scope of
this book, but two of the more common processes, namely
finding the maximum value and sorting some data, will be
briefly examined.

To find the maximum value in an array we need to extract
the first number and treat that as the maximum then search
along the array for a larger value and swap it if one is
found.   Assume that the array N already has twenty numbers
stored in it.

```
1000   REM FIND MAX VALUE
1100   MAX = N(1)
1200   FOR K = 2 TO 20
1300      IF N(K)>MAX THEN MAX=N(K)
1400   NEXT K
1500   PRINT "MAXIMUM VALUE:";MAX
```

The key to this program segment is line 1300, where the new
maximum value is assigned to the variable MAX.

Let us now use the following numbers to develop a means of
sorting data into ascending order.

        10 4 8 7 3 1 2 9

They can be sorted by using the following steps:

         compare two adjacent numbers
         swap them if they are out of order
         record the fact that there was a swap
         keep going until the array has been scanned
         do it all again if there were any swaps.

The program would look like this :

```
 600    DIM A(30)
1000    FOR I = 1 TO 8
1100      READ A(I)
1200    NEXT I
1300    FLAG = 0
1400    FOR I = 1 TO N-1
1500      IF A(I) <= A(I+I) THEN 1800
1600      FLAG=1 : TEMP = A(I)
1700      A(I) = A(I+1) : A(I+1)=TEMP
1800    NEXT I
1900    IF FLAG=1 THEN 1300
9999    END
10100   DATA 10,4,8,7,3,1,2,9
```

At line 1300 the variable FLAG is used to indicate whether
any swaps have been made while the array is scanned.   The
FOR loop counts up to N-1.   The last array variable is
addressed by A(I+1).   Line 1500 checks to see if two
numbers need to be swapped.   Lines 1600 and 1700 swap the
two numbers by temporarily storing one of them in a
variable called TEMP.   Line 1900 checks to see if any
swaps have been made - if there have, then the whole
process is repeated.   This sorting routine is very
inefficient.   There are many ways of improving the
efficiency, but they are beyond the scope of this book.

The final program in this lesson shows a slightly different
use of arrays and also provides a chance to revise some of
the string functions introduced in the last lesson.   The
program will read some text from data lines and count the
number of times each letter occurs.   This process is
interesting because the results are usually very similar
for any text written in English. We know, for example,
that the letter E occurs very frequently.   To understand
how this program works, it is necessary to remember that
the ASCII value of A is 65.   We will use L(1) to store the

number of times A occurs, L(2) for B, and so on, up to
L(26) for Z.   The index will be created by subtracting 64
from the ASCII value of the letter.

```
 600   DIM L(26)                ..... dimension array
1000   FOR I = 1 TO 5           ..... five sentences
1100      READ T$               ..... read a sentence
1200      FOR K=1 TO LEN(T$)    ..... look at each
                                      character
1300         CH$=MID$(T$,K,1)   ..... extract a character
1400         CH=ASC(CH$)        ..... convert to ASCII
1500         IF CH<65 OR CH>90
             THEN 1700          ..... is it a letter?
1600         L(CH-64)=L(CH-64)+1 ..... increase letter
                                      count
1700      NEXT K                ..... next character
1800   NEXT I                   ..... next sentence
2000   HOME                     ..... clear the screen
2100   VTAB 23 : HTAB 1:
       PRINT "ABCDEFGHIJKLMN    ..... print letters
       OPQRSTUVWXYZ"                 along bottom
2200   FOR I=1 TO 26            ..... look at count for
                                      each letter
2300      IF L(I)=0 THEN 2800   ..... skip if no letter
2400      FOR J=1 TO L(I)       ..... L(I) is frequency
                                      for letter
2500         VTAB 23-J:HTAB I   ..... position cursor
2600         PRINT "*";         ..... construct histogram
2700      NEXT J                ..... print next star
2800   NEXT I                   ..... next letter
2900   VTAB 1                   ..... move cursor away
9999   END

10100 DATA "JACK AND JILL WENT UP THE HILL"
10200 DATA "TO FETCH A PAIL OF WATER"
10300 DATA "JACK FELL DOWN"
10400 DATA "AND BROKE HIS CROWN"
10500 DATA "AND JILL CAME TUMBLING AFTER"
```

Run the program with different data.   You can vary the
number of sentences by changing the number in the FOR loop
at line 1000.

Exercises

(a)   Read five numbers from a DATA list into an array, then print the numbers out in reverse order.

(b)   Read ten numbers into an array then print out any numbers which are less than 5.

(c)   Read the following numbers into an array:

    8,1,-5,40,-2,0,1,-2,4,4

then print out the array INDEX of any number which is negative.

(d)   Read the following names into an array then print out all the names which start with S.

SMITH,JONES,BROWN,SALTER,SMITHFIELD,KEEN,BROWN,FIELD

(e)   Adapt the program which finds the maximum value in a list so that it also prints out the position of the maximum value.

(f)   Write a program to find the position of the minimum value in a list.

(g)   Write a program which reads the names of a set of students into one array and their total mark for the semester into another array.   Calculate the average mark then print the names of students gaining an above average mark.

. . . .

Interlude 5

We have already looked at the importance of providing good
documentation within a program. It is also very important
to always set programs out in the same way. The reason for
this is that if an error occurs, say, during a READ
statement then it is likely that a problem exists in a DATA
line. If the DATA lines are always stored on the same set
of number lines, then it becomes easier to track down the
source of the error. Also if a group of people always use
similar number lines then it makes it easier for members of
that group to understand each other's programs. It is
proposed to use a set of elementary guidelines in the final
lesson as an example of what can be done. These guidelines
indicate the purpose for each group of line numbers. The
line numbers have been allocated as follows:

0-499	Titles
500-999	Initialization
500-599	Initialize variables (numeric and string)
600-699	Initialize arrays
700-799	Declare files
800-999	Other initialization (e.g. HGR,HCOLOR)

1000-8999	Main Routine
9000-9999	Close files, other ending routines,
9999	END
10000-14999	DATA statements
15000-19999	Functions
20000-29999	Subroutines
30000	Error handling

These line numbers have been chosen arbitrarily and each
programmer likes to develop his or her own particular
style. The advantages of the approach are that programs
are much easier to read and errors are much easier to
detect. For example, if an error message occurs which
indicates that there is a problem with a subroutine, we
know that the subroutine will be in the range 20000-29999.
If we get an OUT OF DATA error then lines 10000-14999
should be checked, and so on. It should also be noted
that setting programs out in this way reduces the
efficiency, but the sacrifice in execution speed is made up
for by the ease with which errors can be detected.

Lesson 6

Subroutines and Animation

The final lesson discusses the use of subroutines in programs. One particular use of subroutines which is discussed is the setting up of shape tables, which in turn leads to the notion of animated graphics.

A common occurrence in programs is for similar sets of
statements to appear in a number of places throughout a
program.   Consider the following program which draws a
truck made up from four squares.

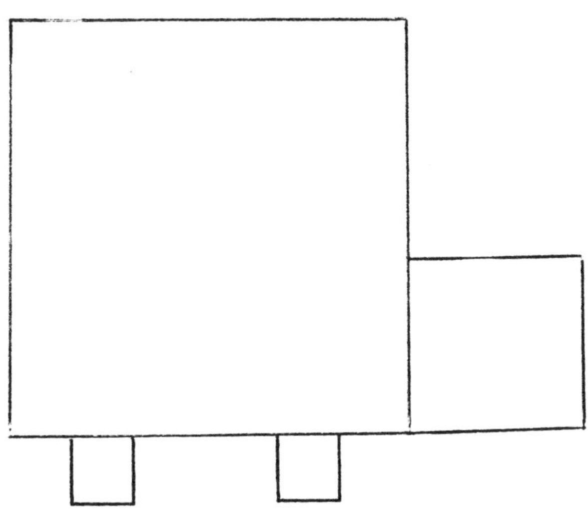

```
100      REM
150      REM   DRAW A TRUCK
200      REM
800      REM   INITIALIZE
810      HGR              : REM TURN ON GRAPHICS
820      HCOLOR           : REM SET COLOR TO WHITE
1000     REM MAIN ROUTINE
1100     HPLOT 100,80 TO 160,80 TO 160,20
         TO 100,20 TO 100,80
1200     HPLOT 160,80 TO 185,80 TO 185,55
         TO 160,55 TO 160,80
1300     HPLOT 115,90 TO 125,90 TO 125,80
         TO 115,80 TO 115,90
1400     HPLOT 135,90 TO 145,90 TO 145,80
         TO 135,80 TO 135,90
9999     END
```

Notice that lines 1100 to 1400 are very similar.   The
Applesoft language allows the one set of statements to be
used a number of times through the use of a SUBROUTINE.

Examine the following program which does exactly the same
as the previous program.


```
100        REM
150        REM  DRAW A TRUCK
200        REM
800        REM  INITIALIZE
810        HGR
820        HCOLOR=7


1000       REM MAIN ROUTINE
1100       X=100 : Y=80 : SIDE=60 : GOSUB 20000
1200       X=160 : Y=80 : SIDE=25 : GOSUB 20000
1300       X=115 : Y=90 : SIDE=10 : GOSUB 20000
1400       X=135 : Y=90 : SIDE=10 : GOSUB 20000
9999       END


20000      REM TRUCK SUBROUTINE
20100      HPLOT X,Y TO X+SIDE,Y TO X+SIDE,Y-SIDE
           TO X,Y-SIDE TO X,Y
20200      RETURN
```


In this program, lines 20000 to 20200 establish a section
of code called a SUBROUTINE which is called from a number
of places in the program.   At line 1100 the variables X
and Y are assigned the coordinates of the corner of the
square and the variable SIDE holds the length of the
square.   The statement GOSUB 20000 asks the program to
execute the section of code starting at line 20000 until
the word RETURN is found.   The program will then return to
the statement following the GOSUB statement.

Therefore the program uses the same subroutine to plot all
the squares by assigning different starting coordinates and
different lengths.   Subroutines are very useful for
reducing the number of lines of code and also for making
the main routine easier to follow.   Another common use is
to enable sections of code written by other programmers to
be included in our own programs.   If the subroutine has
been written correctly, it may not even be necessary to
understand the code in it.

The following program displays a LISSAJOUS pattern by
plotting straight lines from the center of the screen to a
point calculated by a subroutine.   It is not necessary to
understand how the point is calculated in the subroutine.

```
100        REM
150        REM  LISSAJOUS FIGURES
200        REM

500        REM  INITIALIZE
510        SN=2
520        CS=3
530        X=136
540        Y=75

800        HGR   :   REM TURN ON GRAPHICS
810        HCOLOR=3 : REM SELECT COLOR

1000       REM   MAIN ROUTINE
1100       GOSUB 20000 : REM DRAW BORDER
1200       FOR INCR = 0 TO 50 STEP.1
1300           GOSUB 21000 : REM CALCULATE POINT
1400           HPLOT X,Y TO X1,Y1
1500       NEXT INCR
9999       END

20000      REM DRAW BORDER
20100      HPLOT 0,0 TO 279,0 TO 279,159
           TO 0,159 TO 0,0
20200      RETURN

21000      REM CALCULATE NEW POINT
21100      X1=130 * SIN(SN*INCR) + 140
21200      Y1=70 * COS(CS*INCR) + 80
21300      RETURN
```

After the variables are initialized and the screen and
color selected, the subroutine at line 20000 (which draws a
border around the screen) is executed. The section of code
from lines 1200 to 1500 draws approximately 500 lines to
points calculated by the subroutine at line 21000.

Subroutines will now be used as the basis for introducing
one of the most interesting features of the Applesoft
language - SHAPE TABLES. These can be quite complicated to
define so a subroutine which sets up the tables will be
used. (Two further subroutines can be found in Appendix D.)

A shape table can have a number of shapes stored in it.
The shape is displayed on the screen using the DRAW or
XDRAW commands. The structure of the DRAW command is:

        DRAW <shape no> AT <x value>,<y value>

thus

        DRAW 3 AT 140,80

would display the third shape in the table in the center of
the high-resolution graphics screen.   Before the shape is
displayed, two further pieces of information must be
supplied.   The size of the shape is specified using the
SCALE command.   A scale of 1 will cause the shape to be
displayed in its original size. A scale of 2 will cause it
to be drawn double its original size.   The rotation of the
shape from its original position also needs to be supplied.
A rotation of 16 causes the shape to be rotated through 90
degrees clockwise from the original.   A rotation of 32
causes a rotation of 180 degrees clockwise.

The following program displays a square in the center of
the screen.   The square shape is set up in the subroutine
at line 20000. Note that it is not necessary to understand
what is happening in the subroutine provided you understand
that the square is defined there.


```
100        REM
150        REM   DRAW A SQUARE
200        REM

500        REM   INITIALIZE
510        I=0
520        D=0
530        :
800        HGR          : REM TURN ON GRAPHICS
810        HCOLOR=3     : REM SELECT COLOR
820        SCALE=1      : REM NORMAL SIZE
830        ROT=0        : REM NO ROTATION
840        :
1000       REM  MAIN ROUTINE
1100       GOSUB 20000  : REM CREATE SQUARE
1200       DRAW 1 AT 140,80  : REM DISPLAY SQUARE
1300       :
9999       END


20000      REM  SQUARE SUBROUTINE
20100      POKE 232,0 : POKE 233,3
20200      FOR I=768 TO 780: READ D : POKE I,D : NEXT
20300      DATA 1,0,4,0,36,36,63,63,54,54,45,45,0
20400      RETURN
```

Try changing line 820 to SCALE=2 or SCALE=3 to study the effect of that command. The next program changes the SCALE to produce a simple pattern from the squares.


```
100        REM
150        REM   DRAW A PATTERN OF SQUARES
200        REM
500        REM   INITIALIZE
510        I=0
520        D=0
530        :
800        HGR            : REM TURN ON GRAPHICS
810        HCOLOR=3    : REM SELECT COLOR
820        SCALE=1     : REM NORMAL SIZE
830        ROT=0        : REM NO ROTATION
840        :
1000       REM   MAIN ROUTINE
1100       GOSUB 20000   : REM CREATE SQUARE
1200       FOR I= 1 TO 20
1300          SCALE=I
1400          DRAW 1 AT 140,80
1500       NEXT I
1600       :
9999       END


20000      REM   SQUARE SUBROUTINE
20100      POKE 232,0 : POKE 233,3
20200      FOR I=768 TO 780: READ D : POKE I,D : NEXT
20300      DATA 1,0,4,0,36,36,63,63,54,54,45,45,0
20400      RETURN
```


Note that the SCALE takes the values 1 to 20, hence the square gradually becomes larger and larger. Notice also that once the shape has been defined it is not necessary to call the subroutine each time it needs to be drawn. Run the program again but this time move the coordinates to the right and down and then by changing the FOR loop see how many squares can be drawn on the screen before an error occurs.

This idea will now be extended to produce a random pattern of squares on the screen. This will also allow us to revise the INT and RND functions. Twenty squares are drawn at randomly selected positions on the screen. The coordinates at which the square is to be drawn are calculated at lines 1300 and 1400, and the SCALE is set at line 1500.

```
100       REM
150       REM   DRAW RANDOM SQUARES
200       REM
500       REM   INITIALIZE
510       I=0
520       X=0
530       Y=0
540       :
800       HGR            : REM TURN ON GRAPHICS
810       HCOLOR=3       : REM SELECT COLOR
820       SCALE=1        : REM NORMAL SIZE
830       ROT=0          : REM NO ROTATION
840       :
1000      REM  MAIN ROUTINE
1100      GOSUB 20000   : REM CREATE SQUARE
1200      FOR I=1 TO 20
1300         X=INT(279*RND(1))
1400         Y=INT(159*RND(1))
1500         SCALE=INT(20*RND(1)+1)
1600         DRAW 1 AT X,Y
1700      NEXT I
1800      :
9999      END


20000     REM  SQUARE SUBROUTINE
20100     POKE 232,0 : POKE 233,3
20200     FOR I=768 TO 780: READ D : POKE I,D : NEXT
20300     DATA 1,0,4,0,36,36,63,63,54,54,45,45,0
20400     RETURN
```

The next program shows the effect of the ROT command. Two
points need to be made clear before running this program:

* setting ROT=16 rotates the shape through 90 degrees in a
clockwise direction. Setting ROT=32 rotates it through 180
degrees in the clockwise direction. Therefore setting
ROT=8 should produce a rotation of 45 degrees. This will
not happen if the scale is set to 1;

* when the scale is set to 1 only four rotation values
(0,16,32,48) are recognized. As the scale increases, the
number of rotation values increases correspondingly.

In this program a square is stored as shape 1 and a cross
is stored as shape 2. This program rotates the cross to
produce a snowflake effect. The scale is set to 8 to ensure
sufficient rotation values.

```
100       REM
150       REM  DRAW A SNOWFLAKE
200       REM

500       REM   INITIALIZE
510       I=0
520       D=0
530       :
800       HGR          : REM TURN ON GRAPHICS
810       HCOLOR=3     : REM SELECT COLOR
820       SCALE=8      : REM ENLARGE THE CROSS
830       ROT=0        : REM NO ROTATION YET
840       :

1000      REM  MAIN ROUTINE
1100      GOSUB 20000  : REM CREATE SQUARE AND CROSS
1200      FOR I=1 TO 64
1300         ROT=I     : REM SET THE ROTATION
1400         DRAW 2 AT 140,80  : REM DISPLAY SQUARE
1500      NEXT I
1600      :
9999      END

20000     REM  SQUARE AND CROSS SUBROUTINE
20100     POKE 232,0 : POKE 233,3
20200     FOR I=768 TO 789: READ D : POKE I,D : NEXT
20300     DATA 2,0,6,0,11,0,36,63,54,45,0,36,36,36,148,
          18,63,127,73,41,45,0
20400     RETURN
```

Try changing line 1400 to DRAW 1 AT 140,80 and altering the
SCALE to produce a similar effect with the square. Combine
the ideas in the previous two programs to produce random
snowflakes of random size on the screen. You will need to
choose a random value for the coordinate and a random value
for the SCALE for each snowflake.

The two final programs will use the subroutine from
APPENDIX D to demonstrate how animation of shapes can be
achieved. The XDRAW command which draws a shape in the
complement color will be needed to erase the shape. The
concept we will use is almost identical to the technique
used to bounce the ball off the side of the screen in
lesson one. The car will be displayed using the DRAW
command, then erased using the XDRAW command. The car will
then be displayed at the next coordinate, and so on.

```
100       REM
150       REM  MOVING CAR
200       REM

500       REM  INITIALIZE
510       CLMN=0
520       HM=0
530       BM=0
540       I=0
550       C=0
560       :
800       HGR           : REM TURN ON GRAPHICS
810       HCOLOR=3      : REM SELECT COLOR
820       SCALE=1       : REM NORMAL SIZE
830       ROT=0         : REM NO ROTATION
840       :

1000      REM  MAIN ROUTINE
1100      GOSUB 20000   : REM CREATE CAR
1200      FOR CLMN=20 TO 250
1300         DRAW 1 AT CLMN,80
1400         XDRAW 1 AT CLMN,80
1500      NEXT CLMN
1600      :
9999      END

19999     REM CAR SHAPE SUBROUTINE

20000     SCALE=1: ROT=0:HM = PEEK (115) + 256 * PEEK (116)
          : REM POSITION SHAPES AT TOP OF MEMORY
20100     BM = HM - 63: HIMEM: BM:I = FRE (0)
20200     FOR I = BM TO HM - 1: READ C: POKE I,C: NEXT
20300     POKE 233,BM / 256: POKE 232,BM - 256 * PEEK (233)

20400     DATA 1,0,4,0,228,63,39,28,28,63,63,63,63,62,62,
          62,62,62,62,190,45,118,45,32,228,191,78,9,
          45,45,36,36,63,63,103,5,64,73,54,46,45,37,
          141,191,55,54,63,111,9,45,37,12,173,13,53,6,3,
          191,58,7,104,41,0
20500     RETURN
```

Notice that the car now moves across the screen. If you
wish to slow it down, insert a delay loop at line 1350. A
final problem is that of producing animation while other
graphics are on the screen. Consider the following program
which produces some artificial "scenery" which the car
drives past. The scenery in this case will be a set of
vertical lines in the center of the screen.

```
100        REM
150        REM  MOVING CAR WITH 'SCENERY'
200        REM
500        REM  INITIALIZE
510        CLMN=0
520        :
800        HGR            : REM TURN ON GRAPHICS
810        HCOLOR=3       : REM SELECT COLOR
820        SCALE=1        : REM NORMAL SIZE
830        ROT=0          : REM NO ROTATION
840        :
1000       REM  MAIN ROUTINE
1100       GOSUB 20000  : REM CREATE CAR
1200       HCOLOR=2       : REM SET SCENERY COLOR
1300       FOR CLMN=50 TO 150
1400          HPLOT CLMN,40 TO CLMN,120
1500       NEXT CLMN
1600       :
1700       REM NOW MOVE THE CAR
1800       HCOLOR=3
1900       FOR CLMN=20 TO 250
2000          DRAW 1 AT CLMN,80
2100          XDRAW 1 AT CLMN,80
2200       NEXT CLMN
2300       :
9999       END

19999      REM CAR SHAPE SUBROUTINE
20000      SCALE=1: ROT=0:HM = PEEK (115) + 256 * PEEK (116)
           : REM POSITION SHAPES AT TOP OF MEMORY
20100      BM = HM - 63: HIMEM: BM:I = FRE (0)
20200      FOR I = BM TO HM - 1: READ C: POKE I,C: NEXT
20300      POKE 233,BM / 256: POKE 232,BM - 256 * PEEK (233)
20400      DATA 1,0,4,0,228,63,39,28,28,63,63,63,63,62,62,
           62,62,62,62,190,45,118,45,32,228,191,78,9,
           45,45,36,36,63,63,103,5,64,73,54,46,45,37,
           141,191,55,54,63,111,9,45,37,12,173,13,53,6,3,
           191,58,7,104,41,0
20500      RETURN
```

Notice that the car wipes out any graphics that it passes
through. This is because the DRAW command plots the car in
white then the XDRAW command plots it in the complement
color which is black. To overcome this problem substitute
the DRAW command at line 2000 with an XDRAW command. Now,
whatever color the car is passing over, the car will be
plotted in the complement of that color. The second XDRAW
command will restore the original colors.

It is hoped that by now, enough of the fundamentals of
programming and the features of the Apple will have been
covered to allow you to gain any further information from
APPENDIX A or from the manuals supplied by the
manufacturer. Happy programming!

. . . .

Exercises

(a) Use a subroutine similar to the one in the truck
     program to draw a square robot.

(b) Make the robot move across the screen.

(c) Use the square subroutine to fill the screen with
     squares.

(d) Use the square subroutine to produce some patterns of
     your own. For example, you may wish to draw a square,
     rotate it a little then draw it at a larger scale.
     This will produce a shell-shaped pattern.

(e) Display the cross inside the square. You will need to
     increase the scale of the square to do this.

(f) Display a car in each of the four corners of the
     screen.

(g) Display a "parking lot" of cars.

(h) Draw a house on the screen then make the car drive
     past the house.

(i) Make the car accelerate across the screen.

(j) Draw a house on the screen then make the man walk up a
     path, enter the house then stand at the window.

. . . .

Appendix A

Command Summary

In the first appendix all the commonly used commands are described in detail. File handling commands, mathematical functions and some of the more esoteric commands have been omitted.

ASC

EXPLANATION: Converts the first character of a string to
                 its decimal ASCII value.

EXAMPLES: (a) A = ASC ("APPLE")
                 A will be assigned the value 65.

             (b) B$ = "123" : V = ASC (B$)
                 V will be assigned the value 49.

             (c) IF ASC (A$) < 65 OR ASC (A$) > 90 THEN
                 PRINT "ERROR" - check that A$ has been
                 assigned a letter.

HINTS: (a) The value returned is a NUMBER not a
                 STRING.

             (b) Useful for checking errors in data input.

SAMPLE PROGRAM:

                 Write a program to determine the number of
                 surnames which begin with each letter of the
                 alphabet.

```
1000 REM *** ASC DEMO ***
1010 DIM NUMBER(30)
1020    INPUT "NEXT SURNAME:  ";S$
1030    IF S$="ZZZ" THEN 1200
1040    N=ASC(S$) : N=N-64
1050    NUMBER(N)=NUMBER(N)+1
1060 GOTO 1020
1200 HOME : VTAB 4 : PRINT "LETTER";: HTAB 20 :
     PRINT "NUMBER"
1210 FOR I = 1 TO 26
1220 PRINT CHR$(I+64);: HTAB 22: PRINT NUMBER(I)
1230 NEXT
```

EXERCISES:
             (a) Input a name and check that it only contains
                 letters or spaces.

             (b) Write a program which will allow a number
                 of lines of text to be input, then print
                 out a frequency table of letter occurrence.

CALL

EXPLANATION: Allows the user to call a machine code
               subroutine either from a program or in
               immediate mode. The decimal address of the
               start of the subroutine must be specified.

EXAMPLES: (a) CALL -936

               Clears all characters in a text window and
               moves the cursor to the top left corner.

           (b) CALL 62454

               Provides a quick method of coloring the
               high-resolution graphics screen. Uses the
               color last plotted.

HINTS: (a) The memory locations must be in the range
               -65535 to 65535, although this range is
               further restricted on 16K and 32K machines.

           (b) Negative numbers in CALL statements are the
               two's complement representation of numbers
               over 32767. To convert them to positive
               numbers add the negative number to 65536.

               (i.e. CALL -936 becomes CALL 65536+(-936)
               =CALL 64600)

SAMPLE PROGRAM:

               Write a program segment to color the
               high-resolution screen blue.

               1000   REM***CALL DEMO***
               1010   HGR:HCOLOR=2:HPLOT 0,0
               1100   CALL 62454

               Compare this with the alternative method of
               HPLOTing the colors.

EXERCISES: (a) Use a CALL command to scroll text up five
               lines.

           (b) Use a CALL command to clear the
               high-resolution graphics page to black.

CHR$

EXPLANATION: Converts a specified number into an ASCII
                character.

EXAMPLES: (a) A$=CHR$(65)
                A$ is assigned the string "A"

            (b) FOR I=65 TO 90:PRINT CHR$(I);:NEXT
                prints out the alphabet.

HINTS: (a) This command is the reverse of the ASC
                command and is used for converting numbers
                to their equivalent ASCII characters.

            (b) Often used to "trap" input characters.

SAMPLE PROGRAM:

                In data input programs it is often useful to
                be able to return to a MENU option by using
                the ESC key.

```
1000   REM***CHR DEMO***
1010   GET F$ : IF F$=CHR$ (27) THEN 20000
1020   PRINT "NOT ESC" : GOTO 1010
20000  PRINT "ESC USED"
```

EXERCISES: (a) Write a program which will print out a table
               of numbers (from 0 to 127) and their
               equivalent ASCII representations.

           (b) Create   a   coding/decoding   program   by
               converting each letter in a message into
               their ASCII codes and vice versa.

CLEAR

EXPLANATION: This command zeros all variables and arrays
                and sets all string to nulls.   It also
                resets all pointers and stacks.

HINTS: (a) This function is rarely used since RUN
                executes the equivalent of a CLEAR
                statement, although it may be used within a
                program to "clean up" memory.

            (b) The CLEAR statement does not wipe out the
                program in memory.

SAMPLE PROGRAM:

                This program shows the effect of the CLEAR
                statement.

                1000   REM***USE OF CLEAR STATEMENT***
                1100   A=2 : B=3 : A$="CAT" : A(1)=4
                1200   PRINT "BEFORE CLEAR***" ; A,B,A$,A(1)
                1300   CLEAR
                1400   PRINT "AFTER CLEAR***" ;A,B,A$,A(1)
                1500   END

                RUN

                BEFORE CLEAR *** 2   3   CAT   4
                AFTER CLEAR *** 0   0   0

COLOR

EXPLANATION: The COLOR command sets the color to be used
                in subsequent low-resolution graphics plots.

EXAMPLES: (a) 20 COLOR=7
                sets the color to light blue

            (b) 100 P=15 : COLOR=P
                sets the color to white

HINTS: (a) The color codes are:

    0 - black   1 - magenta   2 - dark blue   3 - purple
    4 - dark green   5 - grey   6 - medium blue 7 - light
                                                         blue
    8 - brown   9 - orange   10 - grey   11 - pink
   12 - green   13 - yellow   14 - aqua   15 - white

            (b) The GR command sets the color to black.

            (c) Colors will vary on different television
                monitors.

            (d) Any number up to 255 can be used. If 16 is
                used the COLOR code will be 0, a code of 17
                will give 1 and so on.

SAMPLE PROGRAM:

                Write a program to color the top half of the
                screen blue and the lower half green.

                100   REM***GR DEMO***
                110   GR:COLOR = 2 : FOR ROW = 0 TO 20 : HLIN
                          0,39 AT ROW : NEXT
                120   COLOR=12 : FOR ROW=31 TO 40 : HLIN 0,39
                          AT ROW : NEXT

EXERCISES: (a) Write a program to fill the screen with
               randomly colored blocks.

           (b) Write a program to display each of the
               colors in a vertical line across the screen.

CONT

EXPLANATION: This command causes a program to continue
                execution at the command following the one
                at which it was stopped.

HINTS: (a) The CONT command is very useful when
               debugging a program.   Variable values can
               be examined in immediate mode when the
               program has been halted by a STOP command.
               The CONT command can then be used to
               continue execution of the program.

           (b) Execution commences at the instruction
               immediately following the STOP command or
               after the command being executed when a
               CTRL-C is performed.

SAMPLE PROGRAM:

                The following program shows the effect of
                the CONT command.

                1000   REM***CONT DEMO***
                1100   PRINT "FRED" : STOP : PRINT "BILL"

                RUN
                FRED
                BREAK IN 1100
                CONT
                BILL

DATA

See the READ command.

DEF FN

EXPLANATION: Allows a single line function to be defined by the user.

    (a) 100 DEF FNAREA(X)=3.14159*X*X
defines a function which calculates the area of a circle.

    (b) 100 DEF FNCF(C)=9*C/5 + 32
converts a Centigrade reading to Fahrenheit.

HINTS: (a) The variable used when defining a function is a DUMMY variable. Hence to print out a table of CENTIGRADE to FAHRENHEIT conversions using the functions already defined we could use the following program segment:

```
110   PRINT "C" , "F"
120   FOR CENT = 0 TO 50
130   PRINT CENT, FNCF(CENT)
140   NEXT
```

    (b) User defined string functions are not permitted in Applesoft.

SAMPLE PROGRAM:

Write a program to print out twenty random integers in the range 10 to 20.

```
50   REM***USER DEF FUNCTION***
60   DEF FNR (R)=INT(10+RND(1)*R + .5)
70   FOR I = 1 TO 20
80       PRINT FNR(10)
90   NEXT
```

EXERCISES: (a) Write a program to plot the function

$$f(X)=X^3+X-2.$$

    (b) Use functions to plot a table of the circumference and radius of a set of circles.

DEL

EXPLANATION: Used to DELete a specified range of line
                 numbers.

EXAMPLES: (a) DEL 20,110
                 deletes all number lines from 20 to 110
                 inclusive.

             (b) 40 DEL 1,10
                 deletes lines 1 to 10 inclusive then halts
                 the program.

             (c) DEL 20,20
                 deletes line 20.

HINTS: (a) If used within a program the CONT function
                 will not continue execution.

             (b) A range of line numbers must be specified
                 even if only one line number is to be
                 deleted.   If only one or two line numbers
                 are to be deleted it is easier to just type
                 the line number then press the RETURN
                 button.

DIM

EXPLANATION: This statement is used to define a set of related variables called an ARRAY. The variables thus established are called SUBSCRIPTED VARIABLES.

EXAMPLES: (a) 10 DIM A(20),B$(15)
This statement will reserve a block of 21 subscripted variables which can accept real numbers and a block of 16 subscripted variables which can accept strings.

        (b) 15 DIM BILL(3,4,5)
This statement will establish an array which can accept integers. The array will consist of six "layers" of variables with each layer having four rows and five columns.

HINTS: (a) All arrays contain a zero element. For example the first element in the array B$(15) is B$(0).

        (b) Arrays can be used without the DIM statement if only eleven elements are required.

        (c) All subscripted variables are set to zero by the RUN or CLEAR commands.

        (d) The maximum size of an array is usually limited by available memory, although it should be noted that the maximum number of dimensions allowed is 88.

        (e) A string assigned to an array can be up to 255 characters long.

SAMPLE PROGRAM:

Students can score from 0 to 20 on a test. Write a program to read the marks for 30 students then print out the number of students gaining each mark.

```
1000   REM***MARK ANALYSIS***
1100   DIM MARKS%(20%)
1200   FOR I=1 TO 30 : READ SCRE :
       MARKS%(SCRE)=MARKS%(SCRE)+1 : NEXT
1300   FOR I=0 TO 20 : PRINT I, MARKS%(I) :
       NEXT
1400   DATA 16,4,15,15.10,11,10,3,10,11,4
          ,20,0,0,4,6,11,10,9,8,7,14,15,13
          ,19,20,11,10,9,9
```

EXERCISES: (a) Write a program to read a set of numbers
               into an array, then print the numbers out in
               reverse order.

           (b) Write a program to read a set of names into
               an array, then sort them into alphabetical
               order.

DRAW

EXPLANATION: This command draws a previously defined
                shape at the specified coordinates.

EXAMPLES: (a) 100 DRAW 1 AT 100,120
               displays shape number 1 at the specified
               coordinates.

           (b) 100   CAR=3 : X=50 : Y=40
               110   DRAW CAR AT X,Y
               displays shape number 3 at the coordinate
               50,40.

HINTS: (a) If no coordinates are specified, the shape
               is drawn at the most recently specified
               point.   For example, MAN=1 : HPLOT 100,100
               : DRAW MAN

           (b) If a shape is moved across a picture using
               DRAW commands, it will erase it.   See the
               XDRAW command for a method of overcoming
               this problem.

SAMPLE PROGRAM:

                Write a program which will cause the car
                (the code for which is given in APPENDIX D)
                to move across the screen.

                100 GOSUB 22000 : REM LINE 22000 HOLDS CODE
                                   FOR CAR
                110 FOR I=0 TO 278:DRAW 1 AT 100,I:
                     XDRAW 1 AT 100,I:NEXT

EXERCISES: (a) Repeat the sample program but this time make
               the car accelerate as it crosses the screen.
               HINT: Put another loop between the DRAW and
               XDRAW statements.

           (b) Write a program which will show the man (the
               code for which is given in APPENDIX D)
               bouncing on a "trampoline".

END

EXPLANATION: This statement stops the execution of a
               program and returns control to the user.

EXAMPLES: (a) 1000 END
               When execution reaches line 1000 the program
               will terminate.

            (b) 120 IF X>10 THEN END
               The program will terminate when X becomes
               greater than 10.

HINTS: (a) A number of END statements may be used in
               one program.

            (b) Useful for establishing the main body of the
               program with any subroutines outside that
               section.

FLASH

EXPLANATION: This command causes output to be displayed
               alternatively in white on black, then black
               on white, and so on.

EXAMPLE: 100 FLASH:PRINT"INPUT YOUR NAME":NORMAL
               causes the request INPUT YOUR NAME to flash,
               thus attracting the user's attention.

HINTS: (a) The FLASH command only applies to output
               from the computer.   It does not affect
               characters being typed in, or characters
               already on the screen.

           (b) The FLASH command and the INVERSE command
               can be used to make displays more appealing
               to the user.

SAMPLE PROGRAM:

               Write a program which will display a "MENU"
               of options for file updating on the screen.

```
100    REM***MENU MODULE***
110    FOR I=1 TO 6
120         READ A$
130         PRINT TAB(10);:INVERSE:PRINTI;:
                 NORMAL
140         PRINT"...";A$:PRINT
150    NEXT
160    PRINT:PRINT TAB(10);:FLASH:PRINT"WHICH
       OPTION  :";:NORMAL:GET OPT$
1000   DATA "ADD RECORDS","DELETE RECORDS",
       "UPDATE RECORDS","OUTPUT RECORDS",
       "SORT RECORDS", "FINISH"
```

EXERCISE: Write a program which will print out a
               number of names and birthdates.   Any
               invalid birthdates should flash to draw the
               user's attention to the error.

FOR ... NEXT(TO,STEP)

EXPLANATION: These commands are used to establish powerful loop structures. The variables can increase by one, or the optional STEP command can be used to provide a wide range of increments.
FOR <loop variable> = <initial value> TO <final value> STEP <step value>.

EXAMPLES: (a) 10 FOR I=1 TO 11 STEP 2:NEXT
the variable I will take the values 1,3,5,7,9,11.

               (b) 100 X=1:Y=0:Z=-.2
110 FOR COUNT=X TO Y STEP Z : NEXT COUNT
the variable COUNT will take the values 1,.8,.6,.4,.2,0.
(sometimes floating point calculations may make the final value 1.16415322 E-10 rather than zero!)

HINTS: (a) An integer variable cannot be used as the "loop variable", although integers can be used for the initial value, final value and step value.

               (b) A FOR loop is always executed once. The value of the loop variable is compared with the final value at the NEXT statement. If the final value has been reached, execution continues at the statement following the NEXT statement otherwise the loop is continued. For example,

FOR I=5 TO 4:PRINT I:NEXT

will print the value 5.

               (c) FOR loops may be "nested" inside each other. The maximum number of nested FOR loops allowed is 10.

               (d) Some strange syntax errors may occur with FOR loops.
e.g. FOR I=S TO P will give a syntax error.

(e) The command NEXT may be followed by a loop
    variable. If no loop variable is mentioned,
    the most recent FOR loop is assumed.

SAMPLE PROGRAMS:

(a) This test program demonstrates the order in
    which nested FOR loops are executed.

```
100   REM***TEST PROGRAM***
110   FOR I=1 TO 2
120        PRINT "***"
130        FOR J=1 TO 2
140             PRINT " !!!"
150             FOR K=1 TO 2
160                  PRINT "  ???"
170             NEXT K
180        NEXT J
190   NEXT I
```

(b) See also the programs for DRAW,FLASH and
    COLOR.

EXERCISES: (a) Write a program which will accept any four
               letters (preferably including at least one
               vowel), then print out all possible
               combinations of these letters.

           (b) Write a program which will cause a "ball" in
               low-resolution graphics to bounce across the
               screen.

           (c) Write a program which will produce the
               following pattern of stars.

```
    *
   ***
  *****
 *******
********
```

FRE

EXPLANATION: This command gives the amount of memory which is still available to the user and performs the function of "cleaning up" string space.

EXAMPLES: (a) 1000 PRINT FRE(0)
The quantity of available memory is output.

  (b) 1000 Y=FRE(0)
The expression in brackets is evaluated but has no effect on the value returned.

HINTS: (a) Applesoft does not automatically clean up string space. Strings are stored in the upper part of memory and the variable name and string location details are stored in a table. When a new string is assigned to a variable the pointers are changed and the old string remains. The FRE statement removes all strings which are no longer assigned.

OLD		NEW	
VARIABLE	STRING	VARIABLE	STRING
A$	BILL SMITH	A$	BILL SMITH
B$	FRED SMITH	B$	FRED SMITH
			JAMES SMITH

(b) If a "memory full" condition arises then string space will automatically be cleared up.

SAMPLE PROGRAM:

This program demonstrates the use of FRE.

```
1000   REM***FRE DEMO***
1100   PRINT FRE(0) ; "4 BYTES AVAILABLE"
1110   A$="FRED":B$="CAT":A$="BILL"
1120   PRINT FRE(0); "BYTES AVAILABLE"
```

GET

EXPLANATION: Fetches a single string character from the
                keyboard.   The RETURN key does not need to
                be pressed and the character is not
                displayed on the screen.

EXAMPLE: 100 GET A$
                Execution of the program halts at line 100
                until a key is pressed.   The character
                typed is stored in the variable A$.

HINT: This statement can be used with real
                variables, e.g.:

                        GET P

                however, some strange effects may be noted
                and it is advisable to use the following
                routine if GETing numbers.

                        100 GET P$: P=VAL(P$)

SAMPLE PROGRAM:

                The Apple does not have an INPUT LINE
                command.   This means that INPUT terminates
                whenever a comma is encountered.   This
                program segment will allow long lines of
                text (including commas) to be input.

                100 GET A$:
                     IF A$ <> CHR$ (13) THEN T$=T$ + A$:
                     PRINT A$;:
                     GOTO 100

EXERCISES: (a) Write a program segment which will ask the
               user to input a secret password.   Do not
               print the password on the screen.

           (b) Improve the sample program so that the
               backarrow key can be used to rub out
               mistakes.

GOSUB ... RETURN

EXPLANATION: The GOSUB command causes the program to branch to a SUBROUTINE at the line number given. When the RETURN command is encountered, execution continues at the statement following the GOSUB.

EXAMPLES: (a) 400 GOSUB 20000
410 A=4
The subroutine starting at line 20000 will be executed, when RETURN is encountered line 410 will be executed.

         (b) 100 GOSUB 10:PRINT X
110 A=4
The subroutine starting at line 10 is executed then the PRINT statement is executed.

HINTS: (a) If a section of code is to be repeatedly executed it can be included in a subroutine and placed at the beginning of a program to speed up execution.

      (b) Some programmers place their subroutines after the END statement so that control only passes to subroutines from a GOSUB statement.

SAMPLE PROGRAM:

The following program reads some data then displays an histogram based on that data.

```
100   REM***GOSUB PROGRAM***
110   FOR I=1 TO 10 : READ A(I):NEXT
120   GOSUB 10000:REM HISTOGRAM SUBROUTINE
130   END
10000 FOR I=1 TO 10:PRINT A(I);TAB(5);:
      FOR J=1 TO A(I):PRINT "*";:
      NEXT:PRINT:NEXT:RETURN
```

EXERCISE: Write subroutines which can be used for plotting squares, rectangles and triangles given a starting point X,Y.

GOTO

EXPLANATION: Transfers control to the line number specified. Referred to as an UNCONDITIONAL BRANCH instruction.

EXAMPLE: 10 GOTO 5000
Execution will be transferred from line 10 to line 5000.

HINTS: (a) GOTO statements should be used with discretion. A program with a large number of GOTO statements is hard to "debug" and could also be less efficient than a program with fewer GOTO statements.

    (b) When a GOTO statement is encountered, Applesoft starts at the first line number in the program then checks each line number until it reaches the required one. Hence the use of GOTO statements in long programs causes a decrease in the execution speed.

SAMPLE PROGRAM:

A number of student names and their marks are to be input. As the number will vary from class to class input will be terminated by typing "ZZZ".

```
100   REM*STUDENT MARKS PROGRAM ***
110   DIM N$(30), M$(30)
120   INPUT "NAME ";A$:IF A$="ZZZ" THEN 150
130   I=I+1 : N$(I)=A$:INPUT "MARK :"; M$(I):
          T=T+VAL(M$(I))
140   GOTO 120
```

EXERCISES: (a) Write a program to input a number of household products and their price, then print out the total value.

    (b) Write a program to "bounce" a ball off the side of the screen in low-resolution graphics.

GR

EXPLANATION: This command clears, then "switches on", the low-resolution graphics screen, leaving four lines available at the bottom of the screen for text.

EXAMPLES: (a) 10 GR
The low-resolution graphics screen with four lines of text at the bottom is displayed.

(b) 10 GR:POKE 49234,0
The entire screen is used for low-resolution graphics.

HINTS: (a) Normal low-resolution graphics mode provides 40 rows and 40 columns of points. The top left point has the coordinates 0,0 and the bottom right point has the coordinates 39,39.

(b) The first coordinate specifies the column and the second coordinate specifies the row.

(c) If full-screen low-resolution graphics are used (with the GR:POKE 49234,0 command), then the resolution increases to 40 by 48 (40 columns and 48 rows).

(d) The GR command sets the color to zero (i.e. BLACK). If a PLOT command is attempted, nothing will appear on the screen as the point will be the same as the background color.

(e) If GR is used in a variable name then the GR command may be executed <u>before</u> the message ?SYNTAX ERROR is displayed. Try running the program:

10 GRAPE$ = "SHIRAZ"

Low-resolution graphics will be set then a syntax error given.

SAMPLE PROGRAM:

Write a program to produce colored dots in
random locations on the screen.

```
100 REM***GR DEMO***
110 DEF FNR(R) = INT(RND(1)*R+.5)
120 GR
130 COLOR=FNR(15)
140 CLMN=FNR(39) : ROW=FNR(39)
150 PLOT CLMN,ROW
160 GOTO 130
```

EXERCISES: (a) Repeat the specimen question but this time
put lines of random length on the screen.

(b) Write a program which will draw lines on the
screen which do not cross previously drawn
lines.

HCOLOR

EXPLANATION: The HCOLOR command sets the high-resolution
                graphics color.

EXAMPLES: (a) 10 HCOLOR=3
                sets the color to white

            (b) 100 X=1:HCOLOR=X
                sets the color to green

HINTS: (a) The user will notice that the colors will
                vary considerably among different TV sets.
                The only fixed ones are 0-black, 3-white,
                4-black, 7-white.

            (b) An HCOLOR command <u>must</u> be given before
                plotting starts otherwise the color used is
                indeterminate.

            (c) The HCOLOR command is used for both high-
                resolution graphics screens.

            (d) Legal HCOLOR numbers are 0 to 7.

SAMPLE PROGRAM:

                Write a program to color the screen blue.

```
100 REM***HCOLOR DEMO***
110 HGR : HCOLOR=2
120 FOR R=0 TO 159
130     HPLOT 0,R TO 279,R
140 NEXT
```

                Note: Compare this method with that outlined
                in the CALL command.

EXERCISES: (a) Draw   a   square   on   the   high-resolution
                graphics screen, then color inside it with
                green.

           (b) Display each of the colors on the screen in
                columns.

HGR,HGR2

EXPLANATION: These commands clear the screen to black and then display either page 1 or page 2 of the high-resolution graphics memory.

EXAMPLES: (a) 100 HGR
clears the screen and then displays page 1 of high-resolution graphics.

    (b) 100 HGR2
clears the screen and then displays page 2 of high-resolution graphics.

HINTS: (a) Page 1 of high-resolution graphics leaves four lines of text at the bottom of the screen. The resolution available is 280 (columns) by 160 (rows). The topmost left point has coordinates 0,0 and the bottom right point has coordinates 279,159.

    (b) Page 2 of high-resolution graphics uses the full screen for graphics. No text is displayed. The resolution available is 280 (columns) by 192 (rows). This page of memory is not available on systems with less than 24K of memory.

    (c) Do not use either HGR or HGR2 as part of a variable name otherwise the program will unexpectedly switch to high-resolution graphics.

    (d) If you are using a 32K system be aware that the HGR2 command could wipe out part of the disk operating system. This can cause problems if a user inputs a program then runs it. The HGR2 command wipes out DOS and therefore it is not possible to SAVE the program! The program should be SAVED before it is RUN.

SAMPLE PROGRAM:

See HPLOT command.

EXERCISES: (a) Draw a house with a red roof and blue walls.

            (b) Write a program which will make the man
                 (defined in Appendix D) run across the HGR
                 screen and the car (defined in Appendix D)
                 drive across the HGR2 screen. Switch from
                 one screen to the other to view their
                 progress.

HIMEM

EXPLANATION: This command sets the highest memory location available to a BASIC program. It is used to protect graphics pages, shape tables and the disk operating system.

EXAMPLES: (a) 100 HIMEM:8192
sets the highest memory location available to the start of the high-resolution graphics page. The program now will not overwrite the graphics area.

         (b) 100 HIMEM:16384
Page 1 of graphics can be overwritten by variables but page 2 is protected.

HINTS: (a) The user need only worry about this command if large programs are being written or large quantities of data are being generated.

         (b) To find out where HIMEM is currently set type:

PRINT PEEK (115) + PEEK (116) * 256

since the value of HIMEM is stored in memory locations 115 and 116.

SAMPLE PROGRAM:

This program demonstrates that the memory available to a program is determined by HIMEM.

```
100 REM***HIMEM DEMONSTRATION***
110 HIMEM : 16384 : GOSUB 200 : HIMEM:8192 :
    GOSUB 200 : END
200 PRINT "AVAILABLE MEMORY IS :"; FRE(0) ;
    " BYTES" : RETURN
```

HLIN

EXPLANATION: This command plots a horizontal line of
               points on the low-resolution graphics
               screen.

EXAMPLES: (a) 200 HLIN 4,25 AT 20
               plots a line from 4,20 to 25,20 in the most
               recently specified COLOR.

            (b) 100 FOR I=5 TO 9 : HLIN 10,14 AT I : NEXT
               plots 5 lines of five points each:
               note that this produces a rectangle rather
               than a square in low-resolution graphics.

HINT: If the command is HLIN X,Y AT Z then the
               line will be drawn from coordinate X,Z to
               Y,Z.

SAMPLE PROGRAM:

               See COLOR command.

EXERCISES: (a) Draw a blue horizontal line from 10,20 to
               30,20.

           (b) Draw a block of green points, 10 points wide
               and 8 points high.

HOME

EXPLANATION: The HOME command clears all text within the
       "text window" and places the cursor in the
       top left hand corner.

EXAMPLE: 10 HOME
       clears the screen and sets the cursor to top
       left hand corner.

SAMPLE PROGRAM:

       The following program clears the screen then
       prints a series of messages. The POKE
       commands create a small text window in the
       center of the screen, then the HOME command
       clears the current text window.

```
100 REM***HOME DEMO***
150 HOME
200 FOR I=1 TO 23
250   PRINT"TASMANIA IS A BEAUTIFUL ISLAND"
300 NEXT I
350 POKE 32,10 : POKE 33,15
400 POKE 34,8 : POKE 35,16
450 HOME
```

HPLOT

EXPLANATION: The HPLOT command can be used to plot either a single point, a line or a set of lines on the high-resolution screens.   An HCOLOR must previously have been specified.

EXAMPLES: (a) 10 HPLOT 4,140
            plots a single point at coordinate 4,140.

          (b) 200 HPLOT 20,20 TO 20,120
            plots a straight vertical line between the coordinates specified.

          (c) 150 HPLOT 10,10 TO 10,40 TO 40,40 TO 10,10
            plots a triangle.

SAMPLE PROGRAM:

```
100 REM***COLORED TRIANGLE***
110 HGR : HCOLOR=1
120 FOR I=60 TO 120
130     L=I-60
140     HPLOT 80,I TO 80+L, 60+L
150 NEXT I
160 END
```

EXERCISES: (a) Plot a square starting at coordinate 20,20 then color it green.

          (b) Use HPLOT commands to draw your name.

HTAB

EXPLANATION: This command moves the cursor horizontally across the screen.   It assumes that the line the cursor is currently on has 255 position (forty on each physical screen line).

EXAMPLES: (a) 10 HTAB 20
causes the cursor to move to position 20 on the current line.

        (b) 100 HTAB 130
causes the cursor to jump three lines then move across 10 positions.

SAMPLE PROGRAMS:

(a) File transfers from disk to memory may take quite some time. It is advisable in these circumstances to print a warning message on the screen. Write a program segment to do this.

```
100 HOME:VTAB 12 : HTAB 12 : FLASH:PRINT
"LOADING FILES" : NORMAL
```

(b) The following program will fill the screen with stars (Control C to finish).

```
10 HOME
20 I=INT(RND(1)*39 + 1) : J=INT(RND(1)*23+1)
30 VTAB J : HTAB I : PRINT "*" : GOTO 20
```

EXERCISES: (a) Use the HTAB command to print messages on lines 1,10 and 15 on the screen.

(b) When data are input from a form, it is often convenient to set up the screen in a similar manner to the form. The operator then inputs the information in the same sequence as it appears on the form. Design a program which uses VTAB and HTAB to format the screen for data input.

IF ... THEN

EXPLANATION: The IF THEN statement tests a relationship or logical operator. If it is true the statements following the command THEN are performed otherwise execution switches to the next line number.

EXAMPLES: (a) 100 IF I > 10 THEN 1000
Execution will transfer to line 1000 when I becomes greater than 10.

(b) 100 A=ASC(C$) : IF A > 64 AND A < 90 THEN PRINT C$;"IS A LETTER"
If both conditions are true, the message is printed. If either is false, execution continues at the next line number.

(c) 100 IF A(I) > MAX THEN MAX=A(I) :
FLAG=I : I=I+1 : GOTO 100
If the condition is true, ALL the statements following THEN will be performed.

HINTS: (a) Take care with IF statements in multi-statement lines. If the condition is false execution changes to the next line number. Other statements following the IF statement will not be executed unless the condition is true.

(b) Logical variables are legal:

100 IF I THEN 50

Execution will transfer to line 50 if I does not equal zero (i.e. is true).

(c) Expressions can be used in the condition. For example, if the user wished to test to see if a variable was an even integer, the following statement could be used:

IF I/2 = INT(I/2) THEN PRINT "EVEN INTEGER"

(d) When comparing strings, the ASCII values are used, hence A is less than B and SMITH is greater than BROWN.

SAMPLE PROGRAM:

A data operator is inputting stock control information.   The code number of each item is 4 characters long and starts with a letter.   Write a program segment which will validate the code number.

```
100 INPUT "CODE NUMBER "; C$
110 IF LEN(C$) <> 4 THEN PRINT "INPUT ERROR"
: GOTO 100
120 L$ = LEFT $(C$,1) :
          IF L$<"A" OR L$> "Z" THEN
          PRINT "INPUT ERROR" : GOTO 100
```

EXERCISES:

(a) A set of student names are to be input. When input is complete the terminator ZZZ will be input.   Write a program segment which will test for this terminator.

(b) Write a program segment which will check if a character in a string is a number.

INPUT

EXPLANATION: The INPUT command allows the user to enter
                data from the keyboard while the program is
                executing.

EXAMPLES: (a) 10 INPUT A,B,A$
                A question mark will appear and two numbers
                and a string (separated by commas) may be
                input.

            (b) 100 INPUT "NAME :";N$
                The prompt NAME : will be printed and then a
                string may be input.   A question mark will
                not appear.

HINTS: (a) If a message is to be included in the input
                statement, it must be enclosed in quotes and
                terminated by a semi-colon.

            (b) If a comma appears in an input string, all
                text following it will be ignored and the
                message EXTRA IGNORED will be printed.
                This restricts the free input of text - see
                the sample program for the GET command for a
                method of overcoming this problem.

            (c) If an attempt is made to input a string into
                a numeric variable, the message REENTER will
                be typed and the prompt will reappear.

SAMPLE PROGRAM:

                The students in a class are assigned a
                number from 1 to 20.   Write a program which
                will input the test score for each student.

```
 10 DIM MARK(30)
100 FOR I=1 TO 20
120     PRINT "STUDENT ";I;" ";
130     INPUT MARK(I)
140 NEXT
```

                If the question mark prompt is not required,
                change line 130 to

```
30 INPUT" ";MARK(I)
```

EXERCISES: (a) write a program which will input a number of
               names and ages into two arrays. Terminate
               the process with the name ZZZ.

           (b) Write a program which will ask for the
               number of one cent pieces, two cent pieces,
               etc. up to fifty dollar notes, then print
               out the total amount of money.

INVERSE

EXPLANATION: This command causes output to be displayed
                 as black-on-white rather than white-on-
                 black.

EXAMPLE: 100 INVERSE : PRINT "LOADING FILES" : NORMAL
                 The message LOADING FILES will be displayed
                 in inverse video.

HINT: Remember to use the NORMAL function to
                 restore normal output.

SAMPLE PROGRAM:

                 See sample program for FLASH.

LEFT

EXPLANATION: This function produces a string which is
               formed from the LEFT part of the specified
               string.

EXAMPLES: (a) 100 PRINT LEFT$("TASMANIA",6)
               will extract the left six characters, hence
               printing TASMAN.

           (b) 100 A$="26-APR-1981"
               110 DAY$=LEFT$(A$,2)
               will assign the string 26 to the variable
               DAY$.

HINTS: (a) In the statement LEFT$(A$,N), if the value
               of N is greater than the length of the
               string A$, then all of A$ will be extracted
               but no extra characters will be generated.

           (b) This statement is useful for checking
               responses to questions. The following code
               would allow the responses YES,Y,YEA,YEAH,
               etc.

               ```
               100 INPUT "DO YOU WISH TO PLAY AGAIN";Q$
               110 IF LEFT$(Q$,1)="Y" THEN 10000
               ```

SAMPLE PROGRAM:

               The following program demonstrates the use
               of a variable in the LEFT command.

               ```
               100 REM *** LEFT DEMO ***
               110 A$="ABCDEFGHIJKLMNOPQRSTUVWXYZ"
               120 FOR I=1 TO 26
               130     PRINT LEFT$(A$,I)
               140 NEXT I
               ```

EXERCISES: (a) Write a program which will input a string of
               any length (up to 255 characters) and then
               print out the first letter, then the first
               and second, and so on.

           (b) Write some code which will input a date
               string then check to see if the day is
               valid.

LEN

EXPLANATION: This string returns the number of characters
in a string.

EXAMPLES: (a) A$ = "29-APR-1981" : PRINT LEN(A$)
the length of the string is 11.

           (b) 110 INPUT CODE$: L=LEN(CODE$)
110 IF L <> 6 THEN PRINT "INPUT ERROR"
This code checks that the number of
characters in CODE$ is 6.

HINTS: (a) This function is very useful for validating
input data when those data are of fixed
length.

        (b) Remember that the LEN function returns a
number not a string.

SAMPLE PROGRAM:

This program demonstrates how to erase a
word on the text screen by first finding its
LENgth.

```
100 HOME
110 INPUT WRD$
120 VTAB 10 : HTAB 20
130 PRINT WRD$;
140 FOR DLY=1 TO 200:NEXT
150 HTAB 20 : PRINT SPC(LEN(WRD$))
```

EXERCISE: Write a section of code which will check
that an ISBN has one digit then a hyphen
then four digits then a hyphen then four
digits then a hyphen then a final single
digit. An example is 0-7100-1560-7.

LET

EXPLANATION: This optional command is used to assign
               values to variables (numeric, string or
               array).

EXAMPLES: (a) 10 LET PI=3.14159 or 10 PI=3.14159
               These are equivalent statements assigning
               the value 3.14159 to a variable named PI.

            (b) 20 LET A$="BILL SMITH" or 20 A$="BILL SMITH"
               Either statement assigns the name BILL SMITH
               to the string variable A$.

HINTS: (a) When making an assignment to a string
               variable, the string variable must be
               enclosed in quotes.

               e.g.   100 COST$="12.36"

            (b) An expression or string expression can be
               used to make an assignment.

               e.g. 100 Y=SQR(R 2-X 2)

               or

               100 A$=MID$(B$,4,3)+"/"+RIGHT$(B$,4)

            (c) Statements such as 100 I=I+1 can be thought
               of as "assign to the variable I the previous
               value of I plus 1".

LIST

EXPLANATION: This command is used to list a program on the screen.

EXAMPLES: (a) LIST
         lists the entire program

        (b) LIST 20
         lists line 20

        (c) LIST 100,200
         lists lines 100 through to 200

        (d) LIST,100
         lists from the beginning of the program up to line 100

        (e) LIST 500,
         lists from line 500 to the end of the program.

HINT: Remember that LISTing a program destroys user defined formatting. It is not possible, for example, to indent FOR loops or to provide other internal structure in the program.

LOAD

EXPLANATION: This command LOADs a program into primary
               memory.

EXAMPLES: (a) LOAD
               The LOAD command is used to load the next
               program from cassette tape.

           (b) LOAD INVENTORY
               will search the floppy disk for an Applesoft
               or Integer program called INVENTORY.

           (c) LOAD FRED , S5,D2
               will search for a program called FRED on the
               second disk drive connected to slot 5.

LOMEM

EXPLANATION: Sets the address of the lowest memory location at which a BASIC program can store variables.

EXAMPLES: (a) 100 LOMEM:16384
            protects the high-resolution graphics page from being overwritten by variables.

         (b) 100 LOMEM:24576
            protects both high-resolution graphics pages from being overwritten by variables.

HINTS: (a) Do NOT set LOMEM: above HIMEM: otherwise an "out of memory" error will be generated.

         (b) Do not change LOMEM: after any variables have been generated otherwise these will be "lost".

MID

EXPLANATION: Returns a part of the string which is specified.

EXAMPLES: (a) 100 PRINT MID$("TASMANIA",4,3)
will print the letters MAN.

(b) 100 A$ = "TASMANIA"
110 B$ = MID$(A$,4)
will assign all characters in A$, starting at the 4th, to the variable B$ (i.e. MANIA).

HINT: If the user attempts a MID$(A$,N) and A$ does not contain at least N characters, then a null string is generated.

SAMPLE PROGRAM:

If dates are input in the form DD-MM-YY (e.g. 26-05-81), write a program which will convert them to the form DD-MMM-YY (e.g. 26-MAY-81).   Do not validate the date.

```
100 REM***DATE CHANGER***
110 MNTH$="JAN FEB MAR APR MAY JUN JUL AUG
        SEP OCT NOV DEC"
120 INPUT "DATE:DD-MM-YY";DTE$
130 M=VAL(MID$(DTE$,4,2))
140 M$=MID$(MNTH$,4*M-3,3)
150 PRINT LEFT$(DTE$,3)+M$+RIGHT$(DTE$,3)
```

EXERCISES: (a) Write a program which will input a long line of text then:

(i)   count the number of times each letter occurs;

(ii)   print out each word separately.

NEW

EXPLANATION: This command deletes the program which is currently in main memory.

HINTS: (a) The NEW command should always be given just before entering a NEW program. It destroys the pointers to the current program as well as the variables.

    (b) What the NEW command really does is put zeros in location 2049 and 2050 ($801,$802) so that programs will not RUN or LIST. If after issuing a NEW the program needs to be retrieved, POKE the address of the start of the second line of the program into these locations and reset LOMEM.

NORMAL

EXPLANATION: Resets text output to white-on-black rather than black-on-white (see INVERSE and FLASH).

NOTRACE

EXPLANATION: Turns the TRACE mode off (see TRACE).

ON ... GOSUB

EXPLANATION: Selects a line number then performs a GOSUB
                 based on the value of the expression.

EXAMPLES: (a) 100 ON X GOSUB 1000,1500,2000
                 If X is 1 then execution transfers to the
                 subroutine at line 1000, if X is 2 then
                 1500, if X is 3 then 2000.   If X is any
                 other value, execution continues at the next
                 statement.

             (b) 100 ON INT((P+Q)/2) GOSUB 20000, 20100,
                                      20200, 20300
                 If the expression INT((P+Q)/2) takes a value
                 from 1 to 4, execution changes to one of the
                 line numbers listed.

HINTS: (a) The selected subroutine is executed then
                 control returns to the statement following
                 the ON...GOSUB.

             (b) Care should be taken that the correct line
                 numbers are listed and that each subroutine
                 finishes with a return.

SAMPLE PROGRAM:

                 A file maintenance program will insert new
                 records, search for an existing record,
                 delete a record or print a report.   Write a
                 section of code which will select the mode
                 required:

```
1000   REM***FILE MAINTENANCE***
1100   PRINT"DO YOU WISH TO:"
1200   PRINT "1...INSERT NEW RECORD"
1300   PRINT "2...SEARCH"
1400   PRINT "3...DELETE A RECORD"
1500   PRINT "4...PRINT A RECORD"
1600   PRINT "5...END"
1700   INPUT"WHICH OPTION:";O
1800   ON O GOSUB 2000,3000,4000,5000,6000 :
       GOTO 1100
```

EXERCISES: (a) Write a general purpose "menu" routine which
               uses an ON...GOSUB statement.

(b) One method of moving a cursor around the
    screen is to use the I,J,K,M keys to rep-
    resent up, left, right and down respec-
    tively. Write a routine which translates a
    key-press into a cursor movement, ignoring
    other keys.

ON ... GOTO

EXPLANATION: Selects a line number then performs a GOTO based on the value of the expression. (Very similar to ON...GOSUB except control does NOT return to the next statement.)

ONERR

EXPLANATION: This statement will cause execution to transfer to a specified line number if an error occurs.

EXAMPLE: 1 ONERR GOTO 30000
            If an error occurs, then execution will switch to line 30000.

HINTS: (a) It is not a good idea to insert an ONERR statement until the program has been debugged.

            (b) The statement POKE 216,0 will negate an ONERR and allow normal error messages to be printed.

            (c) The ONERR statement uses the Applesoft stacks so FOR loops or GOSUB...RETURN pairs must be re-executed. If the error handling code returns execution to a NEXT or RETURN, a further error will occur.

            (d) Some problems have been encountered with the error handling routines. To overcome some of these, read the following machine-level routine into memory at the start of the program:

```
FOR I=768 TO 777:READ X:POKE I,X:NEXT
DATA 104,168,104,166,223,154,72,152,72,96
```

            Then in the error handling routine issue a CALL 768.

            (e) Appendix B lists the errors which can be detected by an ONERR statement.

            (f) The error code is stored in location 222 and the line at which the error occurred is stored at locations 218 and 219. To print out the line number use:

```
PRINT PEEK (218) + 256*PEEK(219)
```

SAMPLE PROGRAM:

Write some code which will allow the user to
type in a filename then print out a message
if the file does not exist.

```
100    ONERR GOTO 10000
200    INPUT "FILENAME:";F$
300    PRINT CHR$(4); "LOAD"; F$
  .
  .
  .
10000 REM***ERROR ROUTINE***
10100 ER=PEEK(222)
10200 IF ER=6 THEN PRINT "FILE" ; F$;" DOES
      NOT EXIST"
10300 GOTO 200
```

EXERCISES: (a) Write error handling routines which will
               trap division by zero, type mismatch and
               CTRL-C.

           (b) Write a routine which will print out
               messages of the form:

               ERROR 6 AT LINE 15000

           (c) Using the error code in Appendix B improve
               the last program so that the type of error
               is printed.

PDL

EXPLANATION: This command returns the value of the specified game control paddle.

EXAMPLES: (a) Y = PDL(0)
assigns a value from 0 to 255 to the variable Y, depending on the position of the games paddle.

          (b) PRINT PDL(I) * 50
prints the value of the Ith games paddle multiplied by 50.

HINTS: (a) The legal values of N in PDL(N) are 0 to 3. The use of values outside this range will produce strange results.

          (b) An attempt to read two games paddles consecutively may give incorrect results.

Hence a statement such as:

IF PDL(0) <100 AND PDL(1) <100 THEN 10000

may not work as expected. Use a short delay loop to separate successive readings of the paddle.

SAMPLE PROGRAM:

Use the games paddles to draw lines on the high-resolution graphics screen. Push a button to draw the line.

```
100 REM***DRAW PATTERNS***
110 HGR : HCOLOR=3
120 X=140 : Y=80 : HPLOT X,Y
130   X1=INT(PDL(0) * 279/255)
140   FOR DLY=1 TO 10 : NEXT
150   Y1=INT(PDL(1) * 159/255)
160   IF PEEK(-16286)>127 OR
      PEEK(-16287)>127 THEN
      HPLOT TO X1,Y1
170 GOTO 130
```

EXERCISES: (a) Write a program which asks the user to
               select an object on the screen by moving a
               set of cross-hairs which are controlled by
               the games paddles.

           (b) Write a short routine which checks if the
               games paddles are plugged in.

           (c) Write a program which uses the games paddles
               to control a "lunar lander" as it approaches
               the surface of the moon.

PEEK

EXPLANATION: This function returns the decimal value of the <u>contents</u> of the specified memory location.

EXAMPLES: (a) PRINT PEEK (8046)
prints out the contents of location 8046.

          (b) PRINT PEEK(103) + PEEK(104)*256
prints the program's starting address.

HINTS: (a) It can be used for reading the keyboard. If a key has been pressed, then the following routine can be used to transfer the character into the string A$.

```
100 KEY=PEEK(49152)
110 IF KEY>127 THEN A$=CHR$(KEY-128):
    POKE 49150,0:GOTO 130
120 GOTO 100
```

      (b) Sometimes a non-existent "memory location" can be peeked to cause some physical effect in the Apple. These are the hardware addresses from 49152 to 53247. Hence there is no memory location 49200 but typing PRINT PEEK (49200) will toggle the speaker once. Similarly PEEK(49249), will read the pushbutton switch on the game controller.

SAMPLE PROGRAM:

Write a program which checks if the cursor is about to reach any edge of the screen.

```
100 HRZ=PEEK(36) : VERT=PEEK(37)
110 IF HRZ=0 OR HRZ=39 OR VERT=0 OR VERT
    = 23 THEN PRINT "YOU ARE ON THE EDGE OF
    THE SCREEN"
```

EXERCISES: (a) Write a program which will click the speaker a given number of times.

      (b) Use the PEEK locations for the keyboard to write a simple text input routine without the use of INPUT or GET statements.

PLOT

EXPLANATION: This command causes a small, colored block to be displayed at the location specified.

EXAMPLES: (a) 100 GR:COLOR=6:PLOT 20,2
will cause a blue block to be displayed in the middle of the screen near the top.

           (b) 200 Y=10 TO 30:PLOT 5,Y:NEXT Y
causes a vertical line to be displayed. This could be done more efficiently with a VLIN command.

HINTS: (a) Remember that the GR command sets the color to black. Hence GR:PLOT 15,20 will not produce a visible block as it will plot black on black.

           (b) When using PLOT X,Y the value of X must be 0...39 and Y must be 0...47.

           (c) The normal resolution set by GR is 40 by 40 unless accompanied by a POKE 49234.0. This eliminates the text window and increases the resolution to 40 by 48.

SAMPLE PROGRAM:

      See the GR program.

POKE

EXPLANATION: Stores a byte of information in a memory location or sends a byte of information to an I/O address.

EXAMPLES: (a) 100 POKE 1813,194
stores the decimal value 194 in memory location 1813. This corresponds to the bit pattern 11000010.

(b) 100 POKE 34,10
sets the top margin of the display. Text will now not be stored in the top ten lines of the display. Useful for putting headings on tables.

HINTS: (a) POKE commands should be used with discretion. Many memory locations contain information which is essential for running Applesoft programs. To reinforce this, type up a short program then type POKE 2048,10. The program will not run.

(b) Even nastier would be the following:

FOR I=0 TO 255:POKE I,0:NEXT

This attempts to wipe out all the system variables.

SAMPLE PROGRAM:

This program uses the fact that the text display is copied from the block of memory from location 1024 to location 2047.

```
100   REM***POKE DEMO***
110   INPUT "CHARACTER";A$
120   A=ASC(A$):HOME
130   FOR I=1024 TO 2047
140      POKE I,A
150   NEXT I
```

EXERCISE: Use the POKE "soft switches" to switch between page 1 and page 2 of high-resolution graphics without clearing the respective screen.

POS

EXPLANATION: Returns the current horizontal position of the cursor, giving a number from 0 to 39.

EXAMPLES: (a) PRINT POS(0)
will print the current position of the cursor.

          (b) 100 PRINT:PRINT "POS DEMO";POS(0)
will cause the message POS DEMO 9 to be printed.

HINTS: (a) The POS function is equivalent to PEEK(36).

          (b) The number which is returned is relative to the left hand margin of the screen. Hence, if a POKE 32,X command has been used to change the left hand margin, the results may be confusing.

          (c) When using POS(X) the value of X is irrelevant. Hence POS(0), POS(1) and POS(89) all produce the same result. If using an expression, it is evaluated so a legal number must result.

SAMPLE PROGRAM:

The following program gives a simple example of how the POS command can be used to see if the cursor is at the edge of the screen.

```
100 REM***POS DEMO***
110 HOME
120   VTAB 10
130   PRINT "A";
140   PRINT CHR$(8);" ";
150   IF POS(0)=39 THEN HTAB 1
160 GOTO 30
```

PRINT

EXPLANATION: This command causes characters to be printed on the specified output device.

EXAMPLES: (a) 100 A=2 : B=3 : C$ = "CAT" : PRINT A,B,C$
causes the contents of A,B and C$ to be output on the screen. The value of A will be printed in column 1, the value of B in column 16 and the contents of C$ start at column 33.

    (b) 10 A$ = "TASMANIA" : B$ = "ISLAND"
20 PRINT A$; " IS AN "; B$
causes the message TASMANIA IS AN ISLAND to be printed.

HINTS: (a) A comma moves the cursor to the next tab field. Tab fields are very restrictive. The first tab field consists of columns 1 through 16. The second consists of columns 17 through 32. This tab field is available only if nothing is printed in position 16. The third tab field (33 to 40) is only available if nothing is printed in positions 24 through 32.

    (b) A semicolon causes the tab columns to be ignored. Hence the statement PRINT "CAT";"DOG" would cause the message CATDOG to be printed.

    (c) Any expressions in a PRINT statement will be evaluated. Hence:

10 I=5 : PRINT 2*I+6

will cause 16 to be printed.

    (d) The PRINT statement should be combined with statements such as HOME, VTAB, HTAB, INVERSE, FLASH and NORMAL as well as functions such as TAB and SPC to produce "friendly" output.

SAMPLE PROGRAM:
See FLASH program.

READ ... DATA

EXPLANATION: The READ command searches for a DATA statement then loads the values found into the nominated variables.

EXAMPLES: (a) 10 READ X,Y : DATA 2,3,4
The variable X will be assigned the value 2 and the variable Y will be assigned the value 3.

          (b) 10 FOR I=1 TO 3 : READ A$(I) : NEXT
20 DATA FRED, BILL, JOHN
The string FRED will be assigned to A$(1), BILL to A$(2) and JOHN to A$(3).

HINTS: (a) The READ statement uses a <u>pointer</u> to keep track of the number of DATA items read.

          (b) If the program attempts to read more DATA than there is in the list, an OUT OF DATA ERROR will be displayed. The error can be trapped with an ONERR statement.

SAMPLE PROGRAM:

The code number, number of items and their unit cost are stored on DATA lines. The list is terminated with the value -1. Use these data to print out a simple invoice.

```
100 REM***SIMPLE INVOICE***
110 HOME
120 PRINT "CODE NO"; TAB(9); "NO OF ITEMS";
    TAB(24); "UNIT COST"; TAB(36); "TOTAL"
130 POKE 34,1
140  READ C : IF C=-1 THEN 190
150  READ N,U
160  PRINT C;TAB(12);N;TAB(27);U;TAB(36);N*U
170  T=T+N*U
180 GOTO 140
190 PRINT:PRINT TAB(36); "====="
200 PRINT TAB(36);T
210 PRINT TAB(36); "====="
500 DATA 31650,2,1.40,47860,7,2,32146,17,1
       ,21417,3,2.60,-1
```

REM

EXPLANATION: The REM command is used to insert comments
                into programs to make it more "readable".

EXAMPLE: 10 REM***DEMO PROGRAM***
                No useful processing is done in line 10 as
                it   only   contains   a   message   to   the
                programmer.

HINT: REM statements cannot be followed by other
                statements as these will not be executed.
                Hence:

                10 REM*HELLO* : A=2
                20 PRINT A*3

                will cause 0 to be printed as A has not been
                assigned a value.

SAMPLE PROGRAM:

                The   following   contrived   program   rounds
                numbers to two decimal places.   The REM
                statements help explain the process.

                100 INPUT A   :   REM INPUT A NUMBER
                110 A = A * 100   :   REM MULT BY 100
                120 A = A + 0.5   :   REM ADD .5
                130 A = INT(A)   :   REM TURN INTO INTEGER
                140 A = A/100   :   REM DIVIDE BY 100
                150 PRINT A   :   REM PRINT ROUNDED NO.

                Note: This program could be condensed to:

                100 PRINT A : PRINT INT (A*100+.5)/100

RESTORE

EXPLANATION: This command puts the "data pointer" back to
                  the first data element.

SAMPLE PROGRAM:

The following program reads the data
forever.

```
10 READ A,B
20 PRINT A,B
30 RESTORE
40 GOTO 10
50 DATA 6,7
```

RESUME

EXPLANATION: This command causes execution to continue at
                  the line where an error occurred.

See ONERR.

RETURN

See GOSUB.

RIGHT

EXPLANATION: This function produces a string which is formed from the RIGHT part of the specified string.

EXAMPLES: (a) 100 PRINT RIGHT$("TASMANIA",6)
will extract the RIGHT six characters hence printing SMANIA.

         (b) 100 DTE$ = "26-OCT-81"
110 YR$ = RIGHT$(DTE$,2)
will assign the string 81 to the variable YR$.

HINT: In the statement RIGHT$(A$,N), if N is greater than the length of the string, the entire string will be returned.

SAMPLE PROGRAM:

The following program causes the message "EAT JOE'S HAMBURGERS" to scroll across the bottom of the screen.

```
100 REM***RIGHT DEMO***
150 HOME
200 FOR I=1 TO 40:SP$=SP$+" ":NEXT
250 A$="EAT JOE'S HAMBURGERS"
300 MSG$=SP$+A$
350   VTAB 23 : HTAB 1
400   PRINT LEFT$(MSG$,40)
450   CUT$=LEFT$(MSG$,1)
500   MSG$=RIGHT$(MSG$,39)+CUT$
550   FOR P=1 TO 100:NEXT
600 GOTO 350
```

RND

EXPLANATION: This function returns a real random number in the range 0 to .9999999.

EXAMPLES: (a) Y = RND(0)
Y is assigned the most recently generated random number.

          (b) 100 X = INT (B*RND(1)+A)
X is assigned a new random number in the range A<=X<A+B.

HINTS: (a) RND(0) returns the most recently generated random number.

          (b) RND (positive number) generates a new random number.

          (c) RND (negative number) returns the same number that was returned when that number was last used.

SAMPLE PROGRAM:

        The following program will produce 10 numbers in the specified range.

```
100 REM***RND DEMO***
110 INPUT"LOWER LIMIT";L
120 INPUT"UPPER LIMIT";U
130 FOR I=1 TO 10
140    PRINT INT((U-L)*RND(1)+L)
150 NEXT I
```

ROT

EXPLANATION: This command sets the angular rotation for the next shape to be drawn.

EXAMPLES: (a) 100 ROT=0
Shape will be drawn in original rotation.

(b) 100 ROT=32
The shape will be drawn rotated through 180 degrees.

HINTS: (a) Each rotation of 16 will rotate the shape 90 degrees clockwise.

(b) If the SCALE is set to 1, only four rotation values (0,16,32,48) are recognized. As the SCALE is increased, the number of rotation values increase correspondingly.

SAMPLE PROGRAM:

If a watch's second hand is stored as shape 1 write some code which will cause it to sweep around a clock face.

```
100 REM***ROT DEMO***
105 GOSUB 20000  : REM SET UP SHAPE
110 HGR : SCALE = 8 : ROT = 0 : HCOLOR = 3
120 REM DRAW CLOCK FACE
130 FOR I=0 TO 64 STEP 4
140      ROT = I
150      XDRAW 1 AT 100,100
160      FOR DLY = 1 TO 50 : NEXT
170      XDRAW 1 AT 100,100
180 NEXT I
999 END
20000 REM SHAPE SUBROUTINE
20100 FOR I=16384 TO 16392
20200    READ S : POKE I,S
20300 NEXT I
20400 POKE 232,0 : POKE 233,64
20500 DATA 1,0,4,0,32,32,32,32,0
20600 RETURN
```

RUN

EXPLANATION: This command causes all variables, pointers and stacks to be cleared then execution to begin at the line number indicated.

EXAMPLES: (a) RUN FRED
The program FRED is loaded from the disk then executed.

        (b) RUN 1000
The program which is currently in primary memory is executed beginning at line 1000.

SAVE

EXPLANATION: This command saves the program which is currently in primary memory on a peripheral storage device.

EXAMPLES: (a) SAVE
stores the current program on cassette tape.

          (b) SAVE BILL
stores the current program on the floppy disk under the name BILL.

SCALE

EXPLANATION: This function sets the size of the shape to
                be drawn.

EXAMPLES: (a) 100 SCALE=1
                 Draw shape with original size.

             (b) 100 SZ=2 : SCALE=SZ
                 Draw shape double the original size.

HINTS: (a) If the scale factor is omitted, then the
                 memory location which stores the scale
                 (location 231) may have a strange value in
                 it and hence produce an unrecognizable
                 shape.

             (b) once the scale factor becomes too large
                 (i.e. greater than about 5), most shapes
                 will begin to disintegrate.

SAMPLE PROGRAM:

                 See ROT program.

SCRN

EXPLANATION: This command returns the color of the
               specified low-resolution graphics point.

EXAMPLES: (a) 20 C = SCRN(5,30)
               The variable C will be assigned the color
               code of the point 5,30.

            (b) 30 IF SCRN (X,Y) = 6 THEN PRINT "YOU HAVE
                       FALLEN IN THE WATER"
               Line 30 checks to see if the current
               position is colored blue.

HINTS: (a) Useful for determining if a "player" is in a
               particular region of the screen.

            (b) Take care with the X value, as the Apple
               accepts values up to 47.   If the value 42
               is used then the X value 2 is assumed.

SPC

EXPLANATION: This function is used to introduce spaces into a print statement.

EXAMPLE: 10 PRINT X;SPC(5) ; "DOG"
leaves five spaces between the value of X and the word DOG.

HINT: Can only be used in a PRINT statement. For example, A$=B$ + SPC(6) + C$ would be ILLEGAL.

SAMPLE PROGRAM:

The following program demonstrates the use of the SPC function.

```
100 REM***SPC DEMO***
110 FOR I = 1 TO 20
120     PRINT SPC(I) ; "A"
130 NEXT I
```

EXERCISE: Write a program which will produce a graph from a given function.

SPEED

EXPLANATION: This command sets the rate at which characters are sent to the specified output device.

EXAMPLE: 100 SPEED = 100

HINTS: (a) This command is very useful when printing instructions for students where presenting a whole screen full of instructions at once would not be in their best interest.

    (b) Normal speed is 255. A slow reading speed is 100.

SAMPLE PROGRAM:

This program demonstrates how to change the SPEED.

```
100 REM***SPEED DEMO***
110 HOME : SPEED=100
120 PRINT "THE INSTRUCTIONS ARE"
130   .
      .
      .
200 PRINT "PRESS ANY KEY TO CONTINUE";:GETA$
210 SPEED=255
```

STOP

EXPLANATION: This command causes a program to cease execution at the line number indicated.

EXAMPLE: 100 STOP
Execution will stop at line 100.

HINT: This command is very useful when debugging programs. The program can be STOPped and then the values of particular variables can be printed out.

STR

EXPLANATION: This function returns a string from the
               numeric value passed to it.

EXAMPLES: (a) 100 Y$ = STR$(81)
                Y$ will be assigned the value 81.

            (b) FOR I=1 TO 9 : X$=X$+STR$(I) : NEXT I :
                PRINT X$
                The string 123456789 will be printed.

HINT: This function is very useful for converting
               the results of calculations into strings.
               It is particularly useful when converting
               financial calculations to strings in order
               to format the output.

TAB

EXPLANATION: This function moves the cursor across to the
                 specified column.

EXAMPLES: (a) 100 PRINT "A" ; TAB (20) ; "B"
                 prints the letter A in column 1 and the
                 letter B in column 20.

            (b) 100 PRINT "CAT" : TAB (2);
                 The string CAT is printed, but the cursor is
                 not moved since it is already past column 2.

HINTS: (a) The TAB statement must be used in a PRINT
                 statement.

            (b) TAB moves the cursor from the left margin of
                 the text window.

            (c) If TAB moves the cursor past the right
                 margin, it reappears at the left margin on
                 the next line.

SAMPLE PROGRAM:

                 Plot a pattern of stars on the text display.

```
100 REM***TAB DEMO***
110 FOR I=1 TO 13
120     PRINT TAB(I*3);"*"
130 NEXT I
```

EXERCISE: Print an invoice in neat columns.

TEXT

EXPLANATION: This command sets the screen to full text
mode and places the cursor on the last line
of the screen.

HINTS: (a) This command also resets the text window to
the full screen.

    (b) Normal text mode is 24 lines of 40
characters per line.

USR

EXPLANATION: This function allows the user to pass a
                function to a machine code subroutine.

EXAMPLE: 10 Y=USR(2)
                The value 2 is passed to a machine code
                routine and the result is stored in the
                variable Y.

HINT: The USR function firstly stores the value in
                brackets in the floating point accumulation.
                The control of execution is then transferred
                to the location stored at $0B, $0C.

VAL

EXPLANATION: This function attempts to convert a string
                into a numeric variable.

EXAMPLES: (a) 200 A$="123" : Y=VAL(A$)*5
                The value 615 is stored in the variable Y.

            (b) 150 X=VAL("15XYZ")
                In this example, the value 15 is assigned to
                the variable X.

HINTS: (a) The VAL function converts all numeric
                characters up to the first non-numeric
                character in the string.

            (b) If no non-numeric character is present
                before the first numeric character, then the
                value 0 is returned.

SAMPLE PROGRAM:

                A set of wholesale prices which are stored
                as string must have sales tax of 27% added.
                Write some code which will perform this
                task.

```
100 REM***VAL DEMO***
110    READ PRICE$
120    IF PRICE$="ZZZ" THEN STOP
130    P=VAL(PRICE$)
140    P = P * 1.27
150    PRICE$=STR$(P)
160    PRINT PRICE$
170 GOTO 110
```

EXERCISE: Read a set of birthdates as strings then
                print out the age of each person.

VLIN

EXPLANATION: This command draws a vertical line between
                the two rows indicated.

EXAMPLES: (a) 100 VLIN 5,30 AT 10
                draws a vertical line from row 5 to row 30
                in column 10.

            (b) 100 FOR I=1 TO 30 : VLIN 20,30 AT I : NEXT
                draws a solid rectangle.

HINTS: (a) It is necessary to remember the VLIN X,Y AT
                Z draws a vertical line from ROW X to ROW Y
                in column Z.

            (b) A value of X,Y or Z outside the range of the
                screen will give an ILLEGAL QUANTITY ERROR.

SAMPLE PROGRAM:

                Students can score a mark from 0 to 10.
                Write a program which will allow marks to be
                input and an histogram constructed of the
                number of students gaining that mark.

```
100 REM***VLIN DEMO***
110 GR : COLOR = 2 : DIM N(10)
120 INPUT "MARK-"; M : IF M=-1 THEN 200
130 N(M) =N(M) + 1
140 GOTO 120
200 FOR I = 0 TO 9
210     FOR J = 0 TO N(I) * 2
220         L = I * 4
230             VLIN L,L+3 AT J
240     NEXT J
250 NEXT I
```

VTAB

EXPLANATION: This command moves the cursor to the specified line.

EXAMPLES: (a) 10 VTAB(6) or 10 VTAB 6
moves the cursor to the start of line 6.

           (b) 10 FOR I=1 TO 20 : VTAB I : PRINT "*" : NEXT
prints twenty stars down the left hand side of the screen.

HINTS: (a) The brackets are optional.

           (b) VTAB commands are relative to the screen <u>not</u> the text window.

           (c) Note particularly that the legal values for this command are 1 to 24 NOT 0 to 24.

SAMPLE PROGRAM:

See HTAB.

XDRAW

EXPLANATION: This command draws a shape in the complement of the colors already plotted at those points.

EXAMPLES: (a) 100 DRAW 5 AT 100,120
displays shape number 5 at the coordinates specified.

            (b) 100 CAR=3 : X=50 : Y=40
110 XDRAW CAR AT X,Y

HINTS: (a) If no coordinates are specified, the shape is drawn at the most recently specified point. For example, MAN=1 : HPLOT 100,100 : XDRAW MAN would draw shape 1 at 100,100.

            (b) Because the XDRAW command plots the complement of the colors on the screen, it can be used to move objects across a previously drawn picture.

SAMPLE PROGRAM:

Assume that the binary file PICTURE has a scene created with the graphics tablet and write some code which will move the car across the screen without erasing it.

```
100   REM***XDRAW DEMO***
110   GOSUB 12000:REM CREATE CAR
120   PRINT CHR$(4); "BLOAD PICTURE,A8192"
130   HGR:HCOLOR=7
140   FOR I = 0 TO 278
150           XDRAW 1 AT 100,1
160           FOR PAUSE=1 TO 50 : NEXT
170           XDRAW 1 AT 100,1
180   NEXT I
```

Appendix B

Error Codes

This appendix contains a very brief explanation of each of the error codes which are likely to appear as a result of a programming or operation error.

CODE	MESSAGE	REASON
0	NEXT without FOR	A FOR statement has been used without a corresponding NEXT statement.
1	LANGUAGE NOT AVAILABLE	The language required (e.g. Integer Basic) is not on the diskette.
2,3	RANGE ERROR	A value which is too high or too low has been associated with a DOS command (e.g. disk drive numbers can only be 1 or 2).
4	WRITE PROTECTED	A write-protect tab is on the diskette.
5	END OF DATA	An attempt has been made to READ beyond the end of the file: useful when reading a file of unknown length.
5	FILE NOT FOUND	The filename given in a command such as LOAD FRED does not match any filename on the disk.
7	VOLUME MISMATCH	The wrong volume number has been used.
8	I/O ERROR	Having trouble reading the disk.
9	DISK FULL	There is no more room on the disk.
10	FILE LOCKED	The file has been LOCKED.
11	SYNTAX ERROR	Bad file name or bad syntax in command line.
12	NO BUFFERS AVAILABLE	All available buffers are in use. Some files must be CLOSED.

13	FILE TYPE MISMATCH	The filename is correct but the file type is different: e.g. typing RUN FRED when FRED is a binary file or a text file.
14	PROGRAM TOO LARGE	An attempt has been made to load a file which will not fit in the available memory.
15	NO DIRECT COMMAND	An attempt has been made to use a command such as APPEND, WRITE OR POSITION in immediate mode. These must be used in programs only.
16	SYNTAX ERROR	Incorrect syntax.
22	RETURN WITHOUT GOSUB	A RETURN statement was encountered without a corresponding GOSUB being executed.
42	OUT OF DATA	A READ statement tries to read more data than that which is in the DATA statements.
53	ILLEGAL QUANTITY	A number passed to a function is out of range. Examples would be negative array subscripts or negative numbers in square root functions.
69	OVERFLOW	The result of a calculation was too large.
77	OUT OF MEMORY	Can occur for a number of reasons. All have the effect that no memory is available.
90	UNDEF'D FUNCTION	Reference was made to a line number which does not exist.

107	BAD SUBSCRIPT	Reference was made to an array element which is outside its dimensions.
120	REDIM'D ARRAY	An attempt was made to dimension an array which has already been dimensioned. It can occur if a DIM statement occurs in a loop.
133	DIVISION OF ZERO	An attempt was made to divide by zero.
163	TYPE MISMATCH	String variables and numeric variables have been mixed in assignment statements or expressions.
176	STRING TOO LONG	A string has a maximum length of 255 characters.
191	FORMULA TOO COMPLEX	More than two statements of the form IF <string> THEN were executed.
224	UNDEF'D FUNCTION	A user-defined function was called although it had not been defined.
254	REENTER	A string has been assigned to a numeric variable in an input statement.
255		A control-C interrupt has been attempted.

Appendix C

ASCII Codes

This appendix contains a list of the ASCII codes which have been used throughout this book.

CODE	CHARACTER	CODE	CHARACTER	CODE	CHARACTER
0	CTRL @	32	Space	64	@
1	CTRL A	33	!	65	A
2	CTRL B	34	"	66	B
3	CTRL C	35	#	67	C
4	CTRL D	36	$	68	D
5	CTRL E	37	%	69	E
6	CTRL F	38	&	70	F
7	CTRL G	39	'	71	G
8	CTRL H	40	(	72	H
9	CTRL I	41	)	73	I
10	CTRL J	42	*	74	J
11	CTRL K	43	+	75	K
12	CTRL L	44	,	76	L
13	CTRL M	45	-	77	M
14	CTRL N	46	.	78	N
15	CTRL O	47	/	79	O
16	CTRL P	48	0	80	P
17	CTRL Q	49	1	81	Q
18	CTRL R	50	2	82	R
19	CTRL S	51	3	83	S
20	CTRL T	52	4	84	T
21	CTRL U	53	5	85	U
22	CTRL V	54	6	86	V
23	CTRL W	55	7	87	W
24	CTRL X	56	8	88	X
25	CTRL Y	57	9	89	Y
26	CTRL Z	58	:	90	Z
27	ESC	59	;	91	-
28	-	60	<	92	-
29	-	61	=	93	]
30	-	62	>	94	
31	-	63	?	95	-

Appendix D

Shapes Subroutines

The two subroutines listed in this appendix have been used throughout the book. They have been designed to set up a shape table which can be accessed through the DRAW command.

MAN SHAPE SUBROUTINE

```
20000     SCALE= 1: ROT= 0:HM = PEEK (115) + 256 * PEEK
          (116): REM POSITION SHAPES FILE AT TOP OF MEMORY
20100     BM = HM - 27: HIMEM: BM:I = FRE (0)
20200     FOR I = BM TO HM - 1: READ C: POKE I,C: NEXT
20300     POKE 233,BM / 256: POKE 232,BM - 256 * PEEK (233)
20400     DATA 1,0,4,0,228,156,210,35,12.12,36,220,34,45
          ,45,222,32,4,56,45,7,9,32,196,255,50,38,0
20500     RETURN
```

CAR SHAPE SUBROUTINE

```
20000     SCALE=1: ROT=0:HM = PEEK (115) + 256 * PEEK (116) :
          REM POSITION SHAPES AT TOP OF MEMORY
20100     BM = HM - 63: HIMEM: BM:I = FRE (0)
20200     FOR I = BM TO HM - 1: READ C: POKE I,C: NEXT
20300     POKE 233,BM / 256: POKE 232,BM - 256 * PEEK (233)
20400     DATA 1,0,4,0,228,63,39,28,28,63,63,63,63,62,62,62,62,
          62,62,190,45,118,45,32,228,191,78,9,45,45,36,36,63,
          63,103,5,64,73,54,46,45,37,141,191,55,54
          ,63,111,9,45,37,12,173,13,53,6,3,191,58,7,104,41,0
20500     RETURN
```